THE PREPPER'S GUIDE TO CACHES

HOW TO BURY, HIDE, AND STASH GUNS AND GEAR

by

JOE NOBODY

T. PIKE

Prepper Press

Your Survival Library

PrepperPress.com

CONTENTS

Chapter 1 1

Introduction, History, and Terms 1

A Short History of the Cache 1

What is a Survival Cache? 3

Chapter 2 5

Why Have a Cache? 5

More Than Just for TEOTWAWKI 6

Hiding Weapons 6

Rally Points 9

Going Underground 11

Chapter 3 13

So Many Options 13

As Security Improves, Accessibility Declines 13

Frequency of Access = Less Security 14

Security + Accessibility + Size = Investment 15

Avoiding Authority Increases Complexity 16

What You Plan to Store Impacts Cache Decisions 18

Chapter 4 19

What Should I Stash? 19

How Much Can I Store? 22

Chapter 5 23

Container Selection 23

PVC Pipe 24

Military Surplus 26

Plastic Dry Box 27

Stainless Steel Containers and Canisters 27

Bottles and Jars 28

Purpose-Built Storage Containers 29

Container Color and Other Tips 30

Chapter 6 ....**31**

Preparing Basic Contents 31

Fire 32

Water 33

Food 34

Chapter 7 ....**37**

Mummy Guns 37

Preservation of Your Arms 38

Cosmoline 38

Vacuum Sealing 39

Cosmoline Alternatives 40

Notes on Application 41

Weapons Retrieval 41

Survival Value versus Cash Value 42

Chapter 8 ....**43**

America's Rifle and the Goat Horn 43

More Weapons Preservation Tips 44

Chapter 9 ....**45**

Ammo: Basically Gun Batteries 45

Speaking of Batteries 49

Preparing Batteries 50

Chapter 10 ....**51**

Fighting the War on Water 51

Vacuum Packing 54

Moisture on the Inside 54

Sealing 56

Chapter 11 ....**59**

Stash the Cache 59

Disadvantages of Burial 59

Where Not to Dig 60

Where to Dig.. 63

When to Bury 65

Tips: Retrieval, Checkups, Test-runs, and Site-scouting................................. 66

Digging 66

Chapter 12 71

Alternatives to Burial... 71

    Home Sweet Home 71

    Hidden Rooms 72

Above Ground Options.. 73

Submersion 75

    Submersed Cache Success Story 76

    Mooring 77

    Submersion Tips 77

Chapter 13 79

Deception, Decoys, and Disguise 79

Deception 80

Decoys... 82

Active Deception 83

Disguise 84

Chapter 14 87

Finding Your Cache.. 87

Using Plumb Lines.. 88

Going High Tech 89

Chapter 15 93

Possible Solutions for Urban Dwellers 93

Emergency Caches 94

Conclusion.. 97

CHAPTER 1

INTRODUCTION, HISTORY, AND TERMS

The primary subject matter of this manuscript is offsite survival caches, with an emphasis on subterranean methods. While secret rooms, covert furniture, and other non-burial techniques are addressed, the vast majority of this title involves digging a hole in the right place and properly storing any number of items.

The intended audience includes preppers or any person who wishes to cache critical survival items in the event of a social collapse, grid-down event, or natural disaster.

The basic concept of storing valuable items in a remote, unattended location requires forethought. Security, waterproofing, location selection, and retrieval are all addressed herein.

Authors Joe Nobody and T. Pike utilize their professional, military, and prepping experience to examine every aspect of caching critical survival supplies and equipment.

A SHORT HISTORY OF THE CACHE

Caches have long been employed by resistance forces to hide resources used in waging war. The act of burying weapons and supplies has been used by both guerrilla units warring against oppressive regimes and terrorists challenging mighty armies.

The French used hidden caches in their fight against the Nazi occupation. The resistance implemented a variety of different tactics to hide weapons and supplies sent by the Allies. Those living under the tricolour flag had very little history of private gun ownership, so the accessible arms, post-surrender, were limited to rural farmers' shotguns.

These freedom fighters relied on supplies from the Allies to wage their war. To hide the weapons, the French cached them in a variety of ways, including securing them in bread panniers, hiding them in culverts, and burying them. In fact, history is full of similar methods being invoked by those forces finding themselves on the lower end of asymmetrical confrontations. The subterranean stashing of goods and supplies is actually rather common when smaller forces face mightier foes.

In the latter part of the twentieth century, the Viet Cong taunted American forces using an elaborate form of this tactic: they attacked American forces, broke contact, quickly buried their weapons, and then blended with the population. This tactic was also employed by enemy forces in Iraq and by the Taliban in Afghanistan. The ability to attack American units and then disappear into the masses of noncombatants made fighting them a difficult venture.

The Viet Cong, according to many experts, were the modern day masters of subterranean military operations. Entire bases were constructed underground; no doubt an effort to avoid superior American firepower, both from the air and from ground-based artillery. Their famous spider holes gave our fighting men fits. They were creative experts in storing supplies and even personnel below ground.

Extensive tunnel systems were common. They stored not only weapons, but also food, batteries, radios, and all the critical elements required to wage war. Retaining their equipment was a key to longevity and persistence during a guerilla campaign.

As an infantry Marine who served in Afghanistan, one of our co-authors experienced the frustration of enemy caches first-hand. He observed and learned a variety of guerilla techniques, tactics, and procedures the enemy used when burying weapons and supplies. He writes, "I remember finding my first cache; it was after a long firefight. We had beaten back the Taliban and were pursuing them like dogs. The area of Afghanistan we were in was rural, and most people made their living farming. Piles of hay for donkeys and goats were randomly scattered throughout the fields. One had caught fire from some of our tracers. That was when I spotted the barrel of a PKM machine gun."

That cache was hasty, crude, and ultimately ineffective. During his time in Afghanistan, he would go on to find several more. His squad discovered caches of weapons, explosives, and even black tar heroin. "With as many as we found I cannot even imagine how many we missed."

In the 1940s, the French faced difficulties in caching their equipment, which was partly due to the technology and manufacturing of the time. The containers they used were not particularly waterproof. Those that were metal suffered corrosive effects; their wooden counterparts were prone to rotting. The French would even cache in urban areas, removing bricks in their floors and burying small weapons and replacing the bricks over the stash.

The Vietnamese faced the same problem. While better technology was available, it rarely found its way into the hands of that rural, struggling, irregular force. They faced the same problems as the

French, only a greater scale due to the higher levels of rain and humidity.

The Taliban in Afghanistan used technology that was available to them, which was greatly limited by their geographical location. The rural areas were less likely to employ modern plastics in their caches. They often simply wrapped weapons in tarps and buried them. Pike personally uncovered numerous tank and mortar rounds that had been cached underground without any form of cover or protection. In America we do not face these restrictions and can employ the latest containers and technology to ensure our supplies stay as usable as the day they were stashed.

The successful use of caches has been proven throughout history as an effective method of survival in the worst of times. We may not have a mighty army to wage a revolution against, but caches still have many important uses.

Moreover, history has proved that commodities we value and use every day may become hard to come by before, during, and after certain events.

WHAT IS A SURVIVAL CACHE?

A survival cache is a collection of items stored in a hidden location, to be utilized in the event of an emergency. Survival stashes can contain a variety of items like food, water filtration tools, fire-making equipment, clothes, weapons, ammunition, or anything else you might need in an emergency. The items may change depending on where you live or the time of the year it is, but the tactics for hiding them do not.

The best way to hide a cache is to bury it; it's much easier to search a house than to dig up an entire pasture. Buried hoards are important to the modern prepper for many reasons. Simple food stashes can be lifesavers in the case of natural disasters, the same with medical supplies. Fuel can be stashed along particular routes to facilitate mobility. Guns and ammunition can be hidden so they are undetectable by thieves. Burying "trade items" for long-term survival could also be wise – inventory such as alcohol, tobacco, and precious metals. The number of items is endless and only limited to a person's anticipated needs and means.

If you have a dedicated bug out location, a survival cache along the way can give you the replenishment you need to actually get to safety in a time of disaster. Imagine the situation is dire, and traveling by vehicle is not an option. A one-hour drive turns into a very long walk. Having supplies hidden along your anticipated path means you do not have to carry as much gear, and you will still have access to the necessary basics to sustain life. The concept is the same as thru-hikers traveling the Appalachian Trail who forward supplies to future checkpoints.

Stashing critical items is a particularly smart idea for remote bug out locations. Having someone break in and steal your stockpiles would be tragic. A few caches can hide significant supplies from marauding individuals or scavenging thieves.

CHAPTER 2

WHY HAVE A CACHE?

The need for a survival stash is obvious to those who prepare. The number of scenarios where having a hidden, off-site hoard of critical items that can make the difference between life and death is incalculable.

Many preppers fear post-collapse looters, others expressing concerns over government seizures. Pre-event theft is another legitimate worry. And then there are fire, tornados, earthquakes, forest fires, floods, hurricanes, and other natural disasters. Some people simply don't have the room to store their preps, while other folks merely want to keep their beliefs hidden from unfriendly, prying eyes.

Anyone who has spent time in a combat zone, enjoyed more than casual hunting or camping, or experienced considerable time in the field knows the value of redundancy. Our culture is full of old sayings that support such thinking – adages such as, "Don't keep all your eggs in the same basket." Remember: the *great* outdoors isn't so *great* on equipment. Things break, rust, get lost, or simply wear out. If excessive movement or fighting is involved, these effects are multiplied.

Today, living in an orderly society (for the most part) allows for the storage of our spares, backups, and alternatives in our homes, garages, and rented storage bins. Many of us have insurance to cover losses or the financial wherewithal to replace our survival assets should disaster or some realization of Murphy's Law come our way.

However, these sensible precautions won't do us a bit of good if the world slips over the edge. There won't be an insurance adjuster if things get really bad. My bank probably won't be open, let alone the store where I buy my long-term food supplies. Most likely, the UPS man won't be delivering my spare rifle bolt or case of batteries.

Personally, I believe the chances of a worldwide apocalypse are slim. That's not why I'm a prepper. I learn skills, practice my arts, purchase and make equipment to be independent and as free as our society allows. I walk through life knowing I don't have to depend on anyone or any technology to survive. This core of self-confidence prompts me to help others develop their skills. A few good caches provide an even stronger piece of mind.

MORE THAN JUST FOR TEOTWAWKI

Lately, there has been another threat that seems to be governing our headlines - the abuse of authority by our government. I'm personally not a big conspiracy guy. I have worked alongside, trained with, and been exposed to members of all levels of federal and state agencies. The vast majority of civil servants are just like you and me – men and women who just want to raise their families, serve the community, and maintain a quality lifestyle. A surprising number are preppers themselves.

There are, unfortunately, exceptions.

More and more it seems like the media propagates stories that invoke both fear and ire in my soul. There are few things that enrage a freeborn American more than injustice via the abuse of power. Almost 600 years ago, the Italian political theorist Niccolò Machiavelli wrote a book titled, *The Prince*. Like most classic writings, you can take away many different meanings and philosophical nuances from this work. One such observation from this manuscript is that any authority must respect the ownership of private property above all other things. "A son can bear with equanimity the loss of his father, but the loss of his inheritance may drive him to despair."

Machiavelli understood that most men could deal with almost any injustice more readily than the seizure of their property. And he wasn't just talking about farmland or the contents of a merchant's shop: "When you disarm the people, you commence to offend them and show that you distrust them either through cowardice or lack of confidence, and both of these opinions generate hatred."

Of all the items you might consider caching, firearms are the most controversial, expensive, regulated, and valuable to others if discovered. They could also be one of the primary personal assets an out of control government would seize, outlaw, or restrict.

There are also those who have concerns that go beyond firearms. Many believe that in the case of a nationwide event, local governments might socialize all available assets within their control, including food, medicine, and fuel. If people are starving and resources are limited, a few individual families with hordes of food may find their preparations seized and distributed across the masses.

Even if you're like me and don't believe widespread gun grabs are worthy of concern, there are plenty of other reasons to have a secret store of weapons.

HIDING WEAPONS

It's every parent's worst nightmare. The phone rings just after 2 AM.

The voice on the other end identifies himself as a police sergeant from your town. "Sir, there's been an incident. You son has been arrested on some pretty serious charges. Before I hand him the phone, I would like to verify the address the accused has listed as his primary residence."

The officer reads your address, which is accurate.

In a case of mistaken identity, your offspring has been arrested for an armed robbery. He was in the wrong place at the wrong time and matched the eyewitness description of the culprit.

After rushing to the county jail, posting bond, and losing a night's sleep, you arrive home at dawn to find three police cars parked in front of your home. They have what is often called an "association" warrant. They want any and all weapons from your home. Watching helplessly as they carry away all of your rifles, pistols, and ammunition, you realize your family is now completely defenseless.

You committed no crime. The weapons belong to you, not your son. Yet, the authorities are commonly granted such powers as a preventative measure. The police want to know if you or your children have committed other crimes using that deer rifle or duck gun. They may send off your weapons for ballistics testing, enter serial numbers in a federal law enforcement database, or decide to be obstinate and hold onto your property for months, even years.

Much has been written about the infamous "New Orleans gun grab," which occurred after Hurricane Katrina. As unrest spread throughout the Emerald City, the mayor and chief of police ordered a plethora of law enforcement, National Guard, and even private security firms to seize residents' firearms. Imagine being an unarmed, elderly resident who had remained in his house while gangs roamed the streets, intent upon scavenging whatever they could.

The aftermath of that illegal event adds more justification for having a secret cache. Despite two successful legal actions in the Federal courts by the NRA, many of the seized firearms were never returned to their rightful owners. Others, when begrudgingly handed back, were severely damaged after having been stored in deplorable conditions.

What if a visiting family member decides to sell a little weed to an undercover officer, and they follow him back to your home? Don't be surprised if local law enforcement shows up at your door and confiscates your weapons.

The cops won't care who the guns belong to, or that the arsenal had been acquired legally. In addition to the embarrassment, publicity, and legal fees, you might have to watch the authorities display your AR15 on the local nightly news. "We didn't find any illegal substances, but we took these weapons off the street."

Some confiscations take place under the most bizarre circumstances.

Take the case of a Connecticut resident who called the police to report a theft at his upscale suburban home. As the cops were investigating, they discovered what appeared to be a stockpile of suspicious items, including bomb-making materials.

Needless to say, federal authorities and state police were swarming the retired chemist and former Remington Arms employee's residence. They seized over 270 legally owned weapons and 10,000 rounds of ammunition.

As things turn out, the "suspect" was a Hall of Fame Skeet shooter, collector, and amateur rocketeer. The bomb-making materials were a combination of his rocket fuel and reloading supplies. He also owned two "race cars," which used jet fuel.

The cost of this citizen's time, legal fees, and public humiliation has been significant. Since every criminal in the region now knows about his inventory of firearms, I doubt he will sleep well at night even after his weapons are returned.

Legal entanglements never seem to end well, so naturally they are to be avoided. The problem is you never know who's going to turn on you or for what reason.

There is a well-publicized case of a Ringwood, New Jersey man who had his home searched after his wife told authorities he had made threats during their child custody battle. The cops, using a domestic violence restraining order, seized a collection of WWII firearms, 40,000 rounds of ammo, and other items. One of the weapons was *suspected* of violating New Jersey's assault weapons law, so the citizen was arrested and held on $200,000 bail. As of this writing, the case is unresolved.

Mental health concerns can also be used as justification for the authorities to confiscate your weapons. Does your liberal daughter-in-law believe your survival supplies are "crazy" or "paranoid?" What do you think would happen if she went to the local law enforcement and said, "He's nuts, and the house if full of guns and explosives. You need to do something before he hurts someone."

Police can and do confiscate weapons to "remove a nuisance or possible nuisance," for the public welfare. They must act upon complaints supplied to them, especially when they are represented as a public threat, sometimes with no factual basis.

In other cases, the authorities have nothing to do with the risk to your weapons and supplies.

Fire, for example, is one of my worst nightmares. Gun safes afford some protection, but even with that expensive precaution, water and heat damage can leave you weaponless while the gunsmith is performing repairs. Are you 100% positive that bargain steel blaster-crib you purchased at the gun show will perform as advertised? Will it really handle 1800 degrees for 20 minutes?

Let's not forget financial hardships.

I know a man who lost a lawsuit after an automobile accident. He couldn't pay beyond his insurance company's cap, so the opposing lawyer talked the judge into what is known as a "writ of execution." A few days later, a deputy was at the front door. "I need a list of your assets, sir. Let's start with firearms – do you own any?"

Theft is always an obvious risk. Gun safes afford some protection, as can hidden racks and disguised furniture. They can be expensive undertakings, and still won't defeat a determined thief.

There are also natural and manmade disasters. Earthquakes, tornados, chemical spills, and a host of other events can leave you hungry and unarmed. The headlines are often filled with stories of floods, blizzards, and forest fires. In many cases, there's little, if any, time to gather personal belongings.

This is not to say that a burying a cache of supplies or weapons is a "bulletproof" strategy. As you continue reading, I will urge you to consider how moisture, accidental discovery, and in some cases, severe flooding can destroy a cache just as easily as flames or a bench warrant.

The potential for breaking the law is another area that deserves serious consideration when contemplating the construction of a cache. While I have some level of confidence in my knowledge of local statutes, you should always check with an attorney practicing in your locale as the laws differ across states, counties, and municipalities. Know the rules before you stash any weapons.

If the police, for whatever reason, show up at your door with a warrant, it will most likely be limited to the premises. In that case, an off-site stash wouldn't be a violation.

If an officer asks about any other properties, storage bins, or outside locations where you have personal effects, you could and should invoke the Fifth Amendment and remain silent. Again, you're not technically violating any statute by not answering.

Things get a little fuzzy when it comes to financial disclosures. If the Internal Revenue Service is seizing your personal assets, non-disclosure of a buried cache of weapons would most likely be a crime. The same would apply to those convicted of a felony. If you're ever caught, the penalties can be harsh.

As with most of preparing, you have to make a decision based on your own specific circumstances. It is not the purpose of this book to advise any reader to break the law. Working within the legal boundaries, however, is every citizen's right. Only your attorney can advise you so that you can make a determination regarding the limits of your activities.

RALLY POINTS

In my book, *Holding Your Ground – Preparing for Defense If It All Falls Apart*, I cover the need for rally points. The basic concept is simple: If you and your group (family, friends, or organization) are separated, where will you meet?

While the principle is simple, the implementation can involve much thought and pre-planning, part of which involves a cache.

In summary, the scenarios where this could be a life-saving preparation are many:

- You're pushed off your bug out location.
- Some group members are unable to arrive at the pre-determined location.
- Natural disaster, such as flood, fire, or tornado cause gridlock and make a rendezvous difficult.
- Someone gets lost.

The rally point should be a location that everyone recognizes and can easily find day or night. The old church on the hill, the bridge, school, or radio tower could all be workable examples. Wherever or whatever you determine is the best solution, you should consider having designated supplies at the rally point.

It's only reasonable to assume a rally point will be utilized under duress. You awake in the middle of the night to a rising river and have to get out – now. The wind changes direction and the forest fire blazes over the mountain before you could pack even the bare essentials. A roving band of looters started a firefight and overwhelmed your defense. Someone knocked a candle into the drapes before going to bed.

Your group may be separated, distressed, or require medical attention by the time they reach the location. You may have an armed, hostile foe in pursuit.

Even if you are not concerned with retreat or natural disaster, a rally point can serve other purposes as well.

I have a friend who is extremely cautious about the location of his bug out cabin. Not even his children – more specifically their spouses, know its whereabouts. His instructions to widely scattered family members are as follows:

If it all goes to hell, make your way to the old barn at the intersection of State Highway X and County Road Y. Pull your car behind the building so it can't be seen. You'll find food and water hidden under the brush pile at the northeast corner. God willing, I'll check there every day at sunrise and lead you back to the cabin.

The above example would require a low-risk, easily accessible cache. If accidently discovered, the contents aren't valuable, controversial (such as weapons), or irreplaceable. The instructions are straightforward, so they can be recalled and executed, even under duress.

My personal rally point is an old, abandoned church at the top of the hill. It is just over 3 miles from my bug out location, the elevated steeple easily visible from a considerable distance. Even the smaller children in my group are drilled regarding its location and purpose. "If you get lost – go there. If we are separated for any reason – go there. If you are in danger and can't get back to the ranch – go there."

Currently, living under the rule of law, the cache is simple and inexpensive, consisting of a cheap flashlight, two bottles of water, and a couple of nutrition bars. It is hidden in an easily accessible place and maintained more for practice and training than any actual survival needs.

Should we ever have to use our bug out location after an event, I would not only increase the quantity of food and water, but also include ammunition and medical supplies. Perhaps a knife, something to start a fire, and a higher quality flashlight.

As mentioned before, you should be cautious in the placement of a stash on property that doesn't belong to you. I have no idea who owns the church. Should that current cache be discovered, I don't think it would sound any alarms or cause the owner any hardship. Its inventory includes less than $10 worth of kit.

If things get very bad, then I'm not going to be worried about trespassing charges or the discovery of a hidden firearm causing black helicopters, complete with fast-ropes deployed, to appear overhead.

That current cache, while not overly useful, has accomplished two important preparations. Beyond serving as a training tool, it has proven that our plan is workable. I can augment the contents with confidence later, and that might be the difference between life and death.

GOING UNDERGROUND

Still wondering if creating a cache is worth it? It seems like a lot of work. Not only is it an investment of time and money, but a hidden stash could be exposed to a variety of different elements whether above or belowground. In reality, a buried cache is exposed to fewer elements. As an example, the ground usually keeps a more even temperature.

A properly planned and executed hoard is protected from the most dangerous component – the human element. A cache can be extremely difficult to locate without the thief knowing the location in advance. With a bit of ingenuity, you can make it nearly impossible for anyone to find your critical stores.

Some people may argue that simply hiding items in clever areas around your house is adequate, and there is little doubt this method could be somewhat effective. Others would disagree.

We believe that hiding items is a short-term affair. Secreted supplies should be the provisions you go to first in the case of an emergency. Concealing large amounts of survival assets can defeat the original intent. If I were a thief tearing through your bug out location, the moment I find a hidden item is the same moment I decide to completely wreck everything until I find the rest.

There *is* value in simply hiding some things. My personal bug out bag is somewhat cleverly hidden, with some precious metals, and a few firearms. But I limit the use of basic concealment to the location I permanently occupy. If I cannot see them every day and I don't need immediate access to the equipment or stores, then I don't believe there merely "hiding" them is as effective as a cache.

Burying a cache, by far the most popular option, does require a certain number of precautions. You must account for the effect of weather and prepare to waterproof, and waterproof, and waterproof. Waterproofing is the bread and butter of a successful cache. Inside and out, preventing moisture from getting your supplies is the single most important step in building a remote store.

If you plan on having several reserves in different places, keep them as organized as possible. For example, it might be best to keep non-weapon gear and weapons separate. Having several collections also has its benefits. You'll have lighter, easier to carry caches instead of one bulky, substantial load.

Caching food and water separately has value. Our brains tell us that the two should be organized together as we do in our homes. But consider a case where damage occurs to, or within, a subterranean storage area. For example, water can burst under frigid temperatures and could ruin the container's integrity and the food. Giving some thought to how you organize your stashed supplies will save you some legwork in the long run.

Planning is crucial to the caching process. Determine how many caches you'll need, what you'll store in them, what items are most valuable, when you'll store, how, where, and why. Keep in mind special considerations for your items. Medical supplies and food can expire. Guns can corrode. Gas and oil can degrade. All of the above are the primary topics of this book.

On the surface, any type of stash isn't a complex process. In practice, however, the difference between finding your critical supplies intact and consumable and unearthing worthless junk depends on having the right knowledge and utilizing proper techniques.

Whether you're a seasoned "stasher" or completely new to caching, you always need a certain mindset when considering the possibilities. You'll need to find a balance between your objective for the caches and how to prevent what could happen to them. As repeated throughout this guide, the process is fraught with compromise.

Finally, we recommend that you don't cut corners. If the legwork, research, and labor of caching are beyond your capabilities, put down the book. By failing to properly prepare, you would most likely waste your valuable resources.

CHAPTER 3

SO MANY OPTIONS

When beginning to seriously consider a cache, the first thing most people experience is a bit of analysis paralysis. There are so many options that it's difficult to know where to start.

Above or below ground? A single, large hoard, or multiple smaller stashes? How much should I invest? How difficult will it be to create? What should I include?

In general, I've found the following set of guidelines helpful. These are not rules, as I'm sure there are exceptions. They will, however, hold true in the vast majority of scenarios:

As Security Improves, Accessibility Declines

Or, the more difficult you make accidental/unintentional discovery of your cache, the more problematic it will be to access.

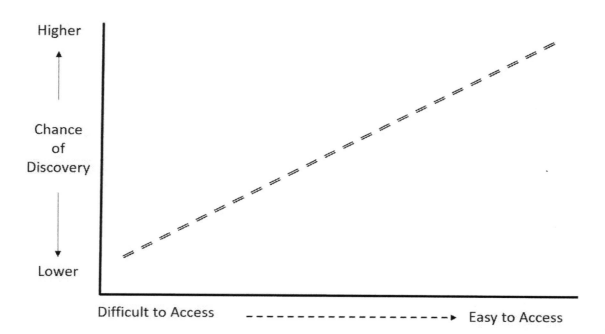

While this guideline is pure common sense, it is often underestimated. If you're storing perishable items or are planning on placing valuable inventory (i.e., firearms or ammo) inside a submerged cache, you're probably going to want to check it periodically.

The simple act of verifying everything is shipshape proposes a risk, as an onlooker could witness your accessing the cache. He might come back later after you've left to satisfy his curiosity. After all, didn't each of us seek pirates' treasure when we were children? Or chase the rainbow's end? Discovery of a cache would surely pose intriguing possibilities for anyone who might happen upon it.

A buried vault has to be excavated, leaving fresh dirt and disturbed surroundings. You could install a trap-door arrangement to make it more accessible, but then that will improve the odds that someone will discover your goodies.

Like so many things in life, caches are a compromise.

This leads us to the second guideline.

Frequency of Access = Less Security

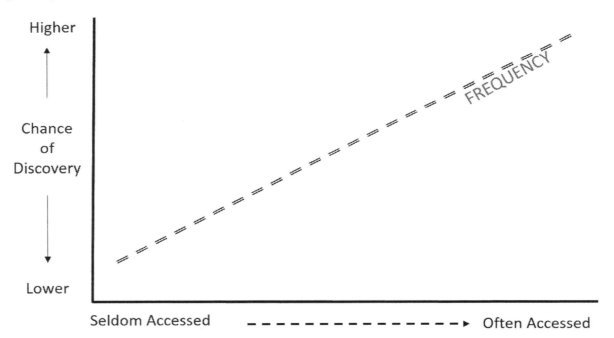

Again, this is only common sense, but something that should be acknowledged as you plan the type, size, location, and contents of your secret warehouses. Digging a deep hole in the middle of a remote woods and burying a PVC pipe filled with supplies is doable, very secure, and would most likely serve your purposes - if you can leave it alone.

I treated my first few attempts at a cache more like an experiment than an actual prep. After about a week, I began to worry about my canister's seal. It rained like the dickens the day after it was entombed. Was moisture getting inside? Did I go deep enough? If water was leaking in, was scent getting out?

Then I was troubled by thoughts of an animal digging up my $300 shotgun after getting a whiff of $20 worth of food. What if a child discovered the weapon inside?

What if I wanted to change the contents? What if later I decided 100 rounds wasn't enough ammo? Your mind can mess with you on so many different levels. In my case, I read an article about caches shortly after my shovel-session. The author included a couple of items I'd never thought about. "I need to dig that up and put those in my store," I concluded.

If you must frequent your stash, approach it from different directions each time. The more times you approach from the same direction, the greater the likelihood your foot traffic will leave a permanent path for the savvy tracker to detect.

Also, take into account that all-important waterproofing. If you're constantly opening and closing any seal, you're taking a risk that materials will wear or that you'll get sloppy and not do a proper job.

Security + Accessibility + Size = Investment

The term investment in this context means time and money. Like any prep, you can take things to an extreme. If you've got the resources, something along the lines of the USAF's Cheyenne Mountain complex comes to mind, or you could fund a nuclear submarine to patrol around underwater and out of harm's way. Silly perhaps, definitely extreme, but the point is made.

There was a time when I considered using a burial plot as a cache location. Ghoulish as it may sound, the concept makes a lot of sense. It's unlikely anyone is going to be digging there until I've passed from this earth, and at that point, I won't care if my cache is discovered.

Since I wasn't going to tell a single soul where my buried treasure was secured, the final-rest-ranch option was the one surefire method that my family would find the stash after I'm dead and gone. Can you imagine the gravedigger's face when his excavator pulls up a chest full of MRE's, an AR15, and 1,000 rounds of ammo in magazines?

My final wishes, however, include cremation. Add to that the facts that some cemeteries now have security cameras, are located in visible suburban areas, and getting caught digging in one might get you arrested, caused me to *pass* on the idea. Having a conviction on my record as a grave robber (shudder) couldn't be a positive life event.

The size of your cache is a factor in this guideline's equation as well. It's only logical that the more you want to bury, hide, waterproof, and camouflage, the more money and time will be required.

Given enough funds and time, anyone could create a nearly impenetrable, well-hidden, easily accessible trove of post-apocalyptic treasures. Where you end up on the scale of secure clandestine versus handy caches depends on your own circumstances and anticipated needs.

Avoiding Authority Increases Complexity

As mentioned previously, some of us may want to create a cache to avoid governmental intrusion, either current-day or anticipated in the future. Burying gold and treasure has been a human tendency since the inception of trade. Mistrust of banks, fear of financial failures, economic collapse… the reasons don't really matter. Hiding things from *the man* has been practiced by everyone from pirates to the colonists fighting the British during the American Revolution.

At first, it may be difficult to imagine a scenario where any federal or local agency would care about your cache of vacuum-packed food and non-restricted medical supplies. Why would they bother?

Before I answer that question, take the following test:

- Do you reload ammunition and thus have gunpowder in your home?
- Do you own a muzzleloader or flint weapon and thus have black powder in your garage?
- Have you ever performed a home improvement project and have nails, pipe, screws, or fittings in your toolbox?
- Do you have a book or box of matches?
- Do you have a can of gas in the garage or bottle of butane camping fuel?
- Do you have more than just a few boxes of ammunition?
- Do you own any military grade firearms, often labeled "assault weapons," by the media?
- Do you own any military surplus gear, such as a load vest, pack, holster, or other warfighting equipment?
- Body armor? Night Vision? Thermal Weapons Sight?
- Do you own any books that address survival, fighting, infantry tactics, explosives, unarmed combat… you name it? The answer here is yes. You're reading this title.
- Have you visited websites that discuss prepping, survival, constitutional rights, or government intrusion?
- Are you a veteran? Do you have combat experience?

If the answer to any four of these questions is yes, an aggressive federal agent with a burr under his or her saddle could arrest you on a variety of terrorism-related charges. An ATF agent once told me, "Practically every home in America has bomb-making materials. We only have to prove intent."

Having a secret survival cache only adds fuel to a circumstantial fire of evidence against the innocent prepper. It's just one more act that can make you look like a bad guy.

Some of you will find your answers to the above quiz are all a resounding, "Yes." I'm probably in even hotter water than most because I have published numerous books on the subject at hand.

These titles, in aggressive prosecutor-speak, could easily be presented as "Rambling, anti-government manifestos."

I wouldn't put it past an overzealous prosecuting attorney to parade your waterproof box of MREs in front of a jury while spouting, "Ladies and gentlemen, the accused has shown a long history of anti-social behavior. This cache of supplies was discovered buried in his backyard, an obvious precaution for a time when the defendant knew he would be trying to avoid capture by the law. It indicates paranoia and proves premeditation."

It just wouldn't look good, no matter how eloquently you explained prepping.

Accusations against you don't have to be associated with your preps. It could be a civil lawsuit, a tax dispute, an accidental discharge of a firearm, the ventilation of a home intruder, or any number of circumstances that point law enforcement's nose in your direction. Your character can be called into question regardless of the originating event. Remember, we live in a time when many believe that the IRS is used to bludgeon those with political differences. These concerns might not be so far-fetched.

Think I'm over the top with this perspective? Perhaps. But, ask any legal expert – the Patriot Act, as well as supporting legislation, is nasty, nasty business if you're on the receiving end. Our elected representatives, with widespread popular support, have given law enforcement some very powerful capabilities in order to fight terrorism. I'm all for that, but, unfortunately, that authority can be abused. It may be rare, but it definitely happens.

There is one primary difference between federal agencies looking for your stash, as opposed to common looters, thieves, or your ex-wife. The government boys can, in extreme cases, utilize a serious arsenal of tools and methods to uncover every stone you've ever trodden upon.

Did you drive to the remote cache location and bury the goodies? Does your bug out buggy have a factory GPS? Chances are, the Feds can retrieve your complete travel history. Even if you don't have such electronics in your car, I bet you took your smartphone along. Cell phone history of your past locations and calls is even easier to retrieve.

Law enforcement personnel are quite good at their jobs, which includes gathering evidence. The average post-collapse looter isn't going to employ a gun-sniffing K-9. Nor will the typical thief be able to retrieve your credit card records and ask what you were doing buying gas just south of Armpit, Texas.

Most crooks don't have access to wall-penetrating radar tracking devices - Federal Marshals do. The Border Patrol can x-ray your entire car in a heartbeat. Microphones and cameras the size of a pinhead are yesterday's technology. We all want that protection against criminals and thugs, but if it's turned on the innocent, bad things can happen.

The authorities can also place enormous amounts of pressure on your friends, employer, and family. Are you and the neighbor still arguing over his dog crapping in your yard? Did you vigorously support the losing candidate in the last sheriff's election?

When I was researching the book, *The Archangel Drones*, I talked with a man who had testified against a police officer in front of a Grand Jury. He eventually moved to a different state, convinced the local cops had revenge in their hearts.

We all have naysayers, and the machine can find them.

The mere fact that you purchased this book could be damning if some DOJ lawyer has taken a serious dislike to you. Internet search history is now as commonly used as fingerprints.

If you're not worried about involvement of the authorities, then you've simplified the entire process of creating a stash. If, on the other hand, you are concerned about governmental overreach, then this title will cover some of the basics of making it harder for *anyone* to find your cache.

What You Plan to Store Impacts Cache Decisions

This guideline addresses more than just the obvious volume of space required for a cache. The type of inventory you plan to stash also plays a factor.

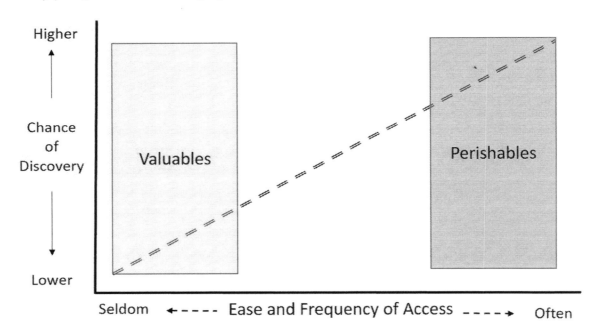

If you're planning to store an expensive rifle, ammunition, and other costly hardware, then you probably want to make a more substantial investment and sleep well at night. These items won't spoil, and your outlay will help avoid the financial sting of someone finding your hide and declaring, "Finders, keepers!"

On the other hand, if the primary inventory is food, fuel, or perishable medicines, then investing in a complex hide probably isn't worth it. These types of goods have to be recycled periodically, so ease of access is more important than long-term concealment. Most likely, their loss wouldn't impact your prepping budget as much as the loss of a weapons/ammunition/precious metals store.

CHAPTER 4

WHAT SHOULD I STASH?

The short answer to "What should I stash?" is anything you don't want someone to find.

In reality, your hoard should be stocked using a little more thought and planning.

The first question should be the intended use of the cache. Is it to sustain travel to a bug out location (BOL)? Is it to support an emergency rally point, or merely as a precaution should something happen to your primary supplies?

I have two different bug out locations, one being 120 miles from my primary, suburban residence, the other over 600 miles distance to West Texas.

Choosing which destination to use involves several factors. During previous Gulf Coast hurricanes, Houston experienced massive traffic jams that blocked every exit route out of the city for hours. If I'm fighting a mass exodus, then my goal is probably the closer BOL.

Hurricanes are relatively short-term events. As soon as the storm passes, we're in a hurry to get back home and survey/repair any damage. That, however, wouldn't be the case if society was collapsing. For a long-term stay, I'm probably going to attempt the 600-mile journey.

Regardless of our objective, I'm very confident in my supplies and kit that would occupy the bed of my truck. I have fuel cans, bug out bags, pre-packed boxes of food, medicine, and ammo. It fills the pickup's bed to the brim.

What happens if my chariot is shot out from underneath me? What if it breaks down or highwaymen overwhelm us and take our cargo? For me, that's always been the worst nightmare. When driving, we are more exposed and vulnerable that at any other time. A cache along each route might be a lifesaving precaution if my family is on foot and completely stripped of our supplies.

Each stash would contain different items, depending on the route. A map of eastern Texas isn't going to do me a bit of good if we're heading west. Water is plentiful around the closer BOL, not so much in West Texas. We wouldn't need food to survive the shorter trek, yet calories out west would be a requirement simply because of the distances involved and the lack of foliage and game to harvest.

Then there's what I call the backup cache or a redundancy store. Spare parts would dominate the inventory here, perhaps for my weapons, mode of transportation, or essential equipment around the BOL.

Geographic location and environment are important, as well. A well-rounded survival cache takes into consideration the prepper's needs, and that often reflects the environment. Hot weather areas need a different inventory than northern, colder regions. Packing a spare rain parka for my West Texas journey would probably would be a waste of space. Anti-venom for rattlesnake bites would be next to worthless in North Dakota.

Do you need spare cold-weather clothing? Are water filters a requirement? Or does the area support an abundance of fresh drinking water? Environmental considerations are an important part of any survival cache.

The census of your group is also worthy of note. Small children can affect the contents to a large degree, as can the elderly. How many people will the cache need to support? Are there any special medicines or other medical needs such as spare eyeglasses?

If you have already gone through the exercise of stocking a bug out location, many of these questions have already been addressed. Often, the proper mixture of cache contents is simply a scaled-down version of what you've already stocked.

What follows is a partial list, included only to seed the reader's thought process. Your inventory will vary, and I'm sure there are numerous important items that aren't listed:

- Weapons, such as a knife, bow, slingshot, etc.
- Firearms
- Cancelation devices (silencers)
- Ammo, bullet molds, and reloading supplies
- Medicine
- Flashlight
- Batteries
- Candles
- Fire starters
- Kindling
- Food
- Water treatment supplies
- Weapon spares and furniture
- Spare/alternative pouches for your load vest (mission configurable)
- Compasses
- Optics (binoculars, weapon sights, BUIS)
- Tents or hammocks
- Automobile parts (oil, spark plugs, etc.)
- A bicycle broken down into parts
- Gun cleaning supplies
- Videotapes
- DVDs
- USB devices, hard drives, CDs, mp3 players, photographs
- Maps to other caches, or just maps
- Currency
- Jewels and jewelry
- Usernames and passwords
- Your Kindle or e-reader loaded with your survival library
- Legal papers, deeds, stock certificates, family trees, receipts, proof you bought supplies recommended in this book (in case you get caught digging it up), **and so much more.**

If you're like many preppers, your bug out bag is never big enough. I'm constantly replacing, reordering, and reshuffling the contents of our "go-packs." Often, after a gut-wrenching process, something has to go due to the physical limits of space and weight.

The "rejected" items often end up in a storage box, never again to see the light of day. That container holding secondary items is a great place to harvest the contents of your first cache.

I'm also fond of buying the latest and greatest. If I see a new gadget that will replace two or more items in my bug out pack, I'll often purchase it for field-testing. Ultimately, a few end up in my pack.

That doesn't mean the replaced items were defective or unusable. Again, the leftovers represent an excellent source of stock for a cache.

HOW MUCH CAN I STORE?

One of the more pleasant surprises I experienced while researching this title was the amount of "stuff" I could stash in a relatively small container. Unlike my bug out pack and load vest, my mind always underestimated how much inventory any given container would hold.

Pictured above is a Mono Vault (more on manufactured products later) model 130s, with a diameter of 9 3/4" and a depth of 23 3/8". That's not such a big tube.

Inside we packed:

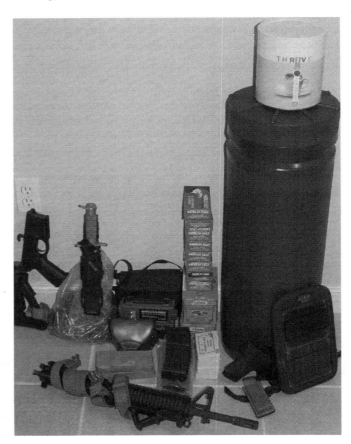

1. Mid-length AR with collapsible stock (upper separated from lower), five 30-round magazines, *and* 925 rounds of 5.56
2. S&W Shield with spare magazine *and* 450 rounds of 9mm
3. Crank-powered radio
4. Large survival knife
5. Pair of binoculars
6. Bag of various "survival" tools (fire-marking products, a few first aid products, etc.)
7. Small solar panels for charging batteries
8. And best of all - 45 servings of a freeze-dried chocolate drink. Yum.

While digging a hole 10 inches in diameter and 30 inches deep isn't what I would describe as a recreational event, it's not a multi-day task either. At least in most soils.

CHAPTER 5

CONTAINER SELECTION

After determining the contents and use of your cache, the next logical step is container selection. With the amount and varieties of vaults available, you should easily find a container to suit your specific needs. When choosing a storage vessel you have to consider all of the items previously discussed, such as contents, accessibility, security, and purpose.

When selecting your container, take the following into consideration:

- Is it completely water and airtight after it's sealed?
- Is resealing an obstacle?
- Does it make any noise when handled (rattling, contents slide back and forth)?
- Is it protected against animals, bugs, bacteria, and other pests?
- Is it resistant to outer damage like abrasions?
- Is it resistant to the elements, such as acidic soil, saltwater, and root growth?
- Can the container endure high amounts of external pressure? A container can warp or change shape, possibly causing the seal to break and damaging the contents.

PVC PIPE

The most commonly used vessel is PVC pipe with sealed ends. While it's entirely up to you which "treasure chest" best suits your caching needs, the absolute best container is one that's non-permeable, corrosion-resistant, and watertight.

For these reasons, PVC pipes are the first choice for many caches. PVC is tough, lightweight, waterproof, meant to be buried, and produces no metallic signature. You can seal the ends with PVC cement, which you can find at hardware stores. PVC is affordable, and it's common enough no one will question what you're planning to do with it. It's unlikely it will become scarce in the days before a total crisis and is available in a variety of sizes from small to large. A piece of PVC about six inches in diameter is perfect for many situations. PVC larger than six inches can be found through pool suppliers.

You can also use an ABS pipe instead of a PVC pipe. These are more damage resistant, though more costly. They're great protection against pests and insects. ABS stands for acrylonitrile butadiene styrene – named after the thermoplastic resin material from which it and its fittings are made. You can find these at hardware and chain stores, as well as online. For sealing, you'll need ABS cement. The brand Oatey is popular and readily available.

There are two downsides to using a "pipe." The first is the diameter. The length can be cut to spec, but for some cache items, the opening's limited size can be an issue.

The second issue with using PVC or other plastic pipe is accessibility and resealing. If you use cement to seal end caps, about the only way to open your cache is with a saw. This is noisy, time-consuming, and difficult to repair.

For the average prepper, the largest individual item will most likely be a weapon, or more specifically, a long gun.

An AR15, sans optics, is just over 8" from rail to the bottom of the pistol grip. This girth can be reduced somewhat by removing the grip and storing separately, but reassembly might be a difficult task when a badly needed weapon is retrieved in the middle of what's been a terrible night.

Most firearms can be broken down for storage, and I have managed to squeeze an AR into a six-inch PVC pipe. If you're not worried about some level of field assembly, re-zeroing sights, and are certain you'll have the required tools at hand, then PVC is difficult to surpass as a subterranean gun safe.

The firearms length is another obvious consideration. Again, given your anticipated situation, skill, and confidence in the availability of tools, practically any blaster can be shortened to the length of its barrel.

Call me paranoid, but my personal decision was to go with a larger container and keep my pain sticks as whole as possible. Visions of trying to unearth firearm-salvation in the darkness, with shaking hands, while possibly being hunted, influenced my judgment.

A variety of weapon configurations have attributes making them more amenable to a limited-space cache, no assembly required. Folding stocks, shortened scatterguns with pistol grips, modular battle rifles, and quick-detach scope mounts should all be considered by the wise prepper.

Unfortunately, many of these selections require an additional investment of your hard-earned money.

In a following section, *America's Rifle and Goat Horn*, we explore various options for stash-guns.

MILITARY SURPLUS

These containers are small, and metal, but also very cheap and available at most surplus stores. A few gun collectors probably have some of these lying around already. These containers are tough and covered in a marine grade olive paint to prevent rust and corrosion. The paint may not last forever, though. These containers are not so much waterproof, but very water resistant, and with a little work can be waterproof. These containers can also be locked, either locked to remain shut, or locked to secure. Also, if you have good seals on your ammo cans, you can put them in a PVC pipe for extra protection for your ammo as long as it fits, plus any other items you decide to include. You can even protect bandoliers of ammo with smaller pipes or with vehicle inner tubes.

The second kind of military container is the larger, heavy, wooden crate. These crates are used to transport mortar rounds or other ordnance and are robust in construction. Wood takes the most work to prepare to be buried. Larger examples can handle extreme weights, but are unlikely to float should a storm wash out your hide. These units are tough and with the necessary preparations, can make a viable vault. They offer a minimal metallic signature, are larger than a standard ammo can, and can be secured with a secondary locking mechanism as well. They can be acquired at most any military surplus store.

A third military container is a U.S. Navy surplus sonobuoy shipping container. These are usually small, anywhere between five inches (13 centimeters) in diameter and three feet long (91 centimeters). They are used to store sonar systems delivered via aircraft. You might need to do some research and extra hunting to find one, as they're not always readily available. There are harder to find, often going quickly when in stock. I would recommend an internet search.

These are perfect-sized containers for caching, but the downside is some of them may need maintenance or repair before using. Some companies that build sonobuoys have piles of rejects below standard, with issues such as defects that can cause leaks or physical molding that isn't quite up to their standard.

However, with an eye for detail to check them carefully and the right supplies, these vessels can easily be repurposed for caching. Tracking one down can be worth your while.

PLASTIC DRY BOX

These commonly available units have similar dimensions to ammo cans. They have a few advantages over metal cans in that many are waterproof, corrosion resistant, and produce no metallic signature. They are not nearly as tough, however, and any locking mechanism is easier to defeat. Available at sporting goods stores as well as many of the retail giants and online, they are typically inexpensive.

A variety of models, shapes, and sizes including actual plastic ammo cans by Plano, are available on Amazon. Many feature an internal rubber lining to ensure waterproofing.

Of the three examples shown in the picture, only one has a watertight gasket around the lid. As you shop for this category of container, you should always look for that feature.

STAINLESS STEEL CONTAINERS AND CANISTERS

You might also consider stainless steel containers and canisters. These containers come in several sizes and are widely available. Because there are a number of varieties, searching via the internet can save a lot of time. Always look for products that are intended to be submerged or buried. Even if your cache will be above ground, the added moisture protection engineered at the factory will provide better long-term service.

Always look for a vessel with an airtight seal. This saves you from applying additional sealants that may or may not be compatible with your vault's materials.

For extra-large, warehouse-scale stashes, consider a steel drum. These are typically used to ship items like grease and oil. You can store a lot of items in them, and your best bet is to order from shipping supply companies. While most common drums lack tight seals, you can order ones with head drums or improvise your own seal. *NewPig.com* has several sizes with head drum seals. However, the larger the drum, the more difficult and laborious it will be to hide or bury. Plan accordingly.

BOTTLES AND JARS

A smaller type of container is a tough sports water bottle. These bottles make great expedient containers, are widely available, cheap, and easy to bury. Perfect for the rushed cache. The water bottle has to be tough. I've found the Nalgene or Camelback brands are plenty robust. These are small and non-metallic, and are perfect for hiding the bare essentials like a lighter, a means to purify water, small med kit, and a knife. A little bottle like this can be perfect to bury around the home with a map of your bigger caches as well. Plus you have a usable container to drink from. An alternative is military flair containers; they may be harder to find. Again, they have the most critical features of an acceptable container – as they are waterproof and hearty.

One last, small option – glass jars. They're cheap, available almost anywhere, and you might even already have a bunch sitting around. They're waterproof, sturdy, and resistant to pests, pressure, and chemicals. The downside is that you'll have to improvise the sealants. Some jars come with a clamp and a rubber washer – while it's watertight, the clamp isn't resistant to corrosion. Jars are great for small, temporary caches. However, if you have a container big enough, you could consider putting a jar inside another cache.

PURPOSE-BUILT STORAGE CONTAINERS

You can purchase a purpose-built storage vessel. One of our favorite examples, the Mono Vault, is essentially a caching container similar in engineering and construction to a homemade PVC pipe contraption.

The tubes come in a variety of different sizes, and all function in the same manner, but for purposes of this guide, we'll experiment with three in particular: the 110s, 130s, and 248s. Each has similar

construction and is available in either black or olive drab. The "s" denotes standard wall construction of 1/4". The tops of the containers have a large-mouth spin-on lid with o-ring seal. On top of that sits another cover, the "Burial Shield," that resembles the top of a landmine in appearance.

I can't speak for everyone, but if I was a looter equipped with a metal detector, I'd think twice about trying to dig one of these up after encountering that shield.

These are robust units, with the manufacturer's web page showing trucks and tractors rolling over the tube and resting on the lip. The variety of shapes and sizes provides excellent options for the prepper who wants multiple caches (and ideally, you would), so you can store practically anything.

In addition to the example shown above, we tested two others.

To provide some reference to the reader, we packed the following into the 248s (diameter of 12 1/4"and a depth of 45") model:

1. Mid-length AR with collapsible stock, five 30-round magazines, *and* 1,075 rounds of 5.56,
2. Ruger 10/22 *and* 1,275 rounds of .22lr,
3. Remington 870 shotgun *and* eighty 12-gauge shotgun shells,
4. S&W Shield with spare magazine *and* 450 rounds of 9mm,
5. A crank-powered radio,
6. A large survival knife,
7. A small pair of binoculars,
8. A small bag of various "survival" tools (fire-marking products, few first aid products, etc.),
9. A small solar panel for charging batteries
10. 45 servings of freeze-dried chocolate drink.

We didn't even take the ammo out of the boxes, which would have provided additional space.

Even the smallest unit, the 110s (9 3/4" and an inside depth of 7 1/2"), provided a surprising amount of storage, allowing an S&W Shield with a spare magazine, 100 rounds of 9mm, and 45 servings of our opulent chocolate drink.

The larger Mono Vaults can be useful for weapons caches to store your rifles and shotguns. Smaller sizes are great for pistols plus other small valuables, if the room allows. There are Mono Vaults specifically for firearms caching, as well. These units are available from numerous online retailers, as well as traditional brick and mortar stores.

There are other products similar in nature available, but as of this writing, the authors have only tested this specific brand.

One word of advice when purchasing any cache supplies – use cash or a pre-paid, anonymous gift or debit card if you don't want to leave a very traceable, financial trail.

CONTAINER COLOR AND OTHER TIPS

I advise against brightly colored containers, such as white PVC pipe. If burying, there's always the possibility of erosion, unearthing by animals, or other exposures. If hiding on a rooftop or inside a structure, you want to use every available bit of camouflage available. A brightly colored vessel would be like a neon sign in the desert, advertising your valuables.

If you reside in a rural area, take a drive to a different town to purchase supplies. Large urban stores, with higher levels of customer traffic, reduce the likelihood of a clerk or shopkeeper remembering your face, or talking to his beer buddies about what "Ol' Joe is up to."

If at all possible, don't give away your intent by purchasing specific quantities or lengths. PVC pipe, for example, is often cut to length by various suppliers. If it's only a few dollars more to purchase your tube in a standard length, in the long run, it might be a worthwhile investment. Be stealthy - If purchasing paint, don't ask the clerk, "Will this brand withstand being buried for 10 years if I spray it on plastic pipe?"

CHAPTER 6

PREPARING BASIC CONTENTS

It would be impossible to provide an all-encompassing list of what gear you as an individual are going to need to survive. As stated earlier, different people and different environments determine that inventory. There are, however, some items that will be relatively common to most any hoard. What follows is a list of the essential items and how to prepare them for extended storage.

At a basic level, the principles of ensuring a long shelf life for your cache are similar to that of survival clothing – employ multiple layers of protection.

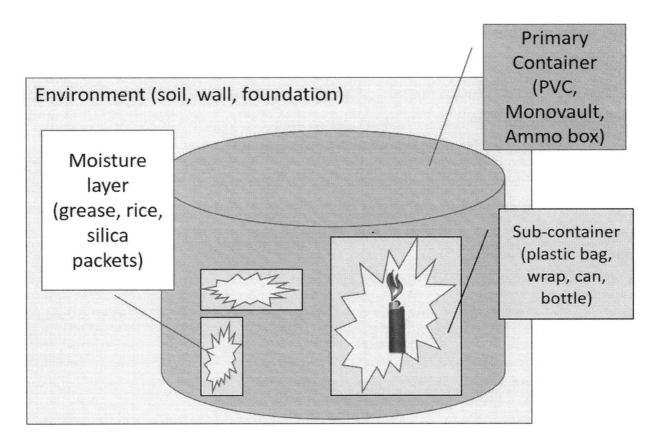

As the chart above indicates, we have several different barriers or obstacles to animals, moisture, corrosion, and other cache-killing effects.

The hoard's first layer of protection should be its surroundings. Since most will be buried, this barrier would be the soil, dirt, or sand.

The next line of defense is the container. In addition to providing overall protection against the elements, it might also have to withstand pressure as well as keep the contents from drifting apart. It may serve to carry your gear away from the hole or stash location.

Then come the sub-containers, which may be plastic bags, tarps, or tin cans.

The fourth layer could be silica packs, grease, rice, or other moisture absorbing substances inside the containers.

To reiterate, humidity, water, and moisture are your cache's second worst enemies; people are the first.

Even if your specific contents aren't addressed in this guide, the methods and techniques that follow are intended to provide examples that will work with most any stashed items.

We will begin with the big three: Fire, Food, and Water.

Fire

Every prepper knows the value of fire. It has been critical to man since the dawn of time. Fire granted man warmth and protection in the night and provided him light to work longer hours. Fire is a natural technology if you will, that has propelled man throughout time and still plays a critical role in the day-to-day life of people.

Fire is essential to survival, for light, warmth, to cook, and to purify water. Having multiple ways to make fire is always wise. Disposable lighters are cheap, and a $10 investment can get you quite a few of them. I always go for the name brands like BIC; they tend to be more reliable than the dollar store specials.

Besides disposable lighters, a good Zippo is an awesome extra. Throw in some spare flints and a few fuel refills, and you will have a long lasting, reliable source of fire. Zippos are made to last; they are tough and rust resistant. I carried one through two deployments, and it still works like the day I bought it. As a precaution, I'd store it the same way I'd store a cheap BIC. Better safe than sorry, right?

If you choose matches, I suggest NATO standard matches. They come in a waterproof plastic container with a built in strike surface. These matches burn like a flare for about ten seconds. And during these ten seconds they are completely windproof and even rainproof. They sell for around $4 per 25. This is on the expensive side for matches, but their performance in a survival situation is unparalleled.

Next, consider flint fire starters, which are near perfect supplies to be housed underground. Magnesium flint fire starters work great whether they are wet or dry. They last a long time, but maybe not forever, so pack a few of these. They take practice to master, but it's an incredibly valuable skill to have. They require some kind of tinder to ignite. Dry leaves, moss, and pine needles work well.

You can make your own tinder easily enough, and with two small and cheap items that are easy to bury. Buy a jar of Vaseline and some cotton balls, cover the cotton balls in the Vaseline, but do not use too much. Over-soaking the cotton balls will render them ineffective. Practice this; find the right amount of Vaseline for ignition while time is on your side. After you master this, I would suggest storing these items separately, so you can make tinder at your convenience.

Another product that has three uses is corn chips. The first is obviously a source of food, the second is as a trade item since they have little nutritional value, and third, they make great tinder. Believe it or not, corn chips make a great fire, and they burn for extended periods.

Solid fuel tablets, sometimes called Esbit or Hexamine cubes, are another inexpensive tinder that is excellent for caches. They have a long shelf life, take up very little space, and burn for 10-12 minutes at 1400 F. I especially appreciate these little jewels when all of the surrounding fuel is soaked and difficult to ignite. They can be used either as a primary source for cooking and heating or as tinder to dry out larger logs. Best of all, they produce no smoke, which might be important in an apocalyptic scenario.

Candles are another basic, foolproof item that should be considered for any cache. Batteries corrode and are extremely susceptible to moisture and time. Wicks and wax are not.

The camping sections of most outdoor and sporting goods outlets have dozens and dozens of various fire-starters. Some require practice and skill, others are as simple as flicking a button.

If you're new to prepping or the survival mindset, I cannot stress enough the importance of fire. You should plan multiple methods to start a blaze that are inexpensive and require little space. Arguably, these are the most important items in any emergency store. I would go as far as to suggest putting lighters, matches, and flint in every cache you make regardless of what else is in it.

Place these types of items in plastic bags and use gorilla tape to guarantee the tops are sealed. Inside the bag, use some kind of a moisture absorber. Silica gel packets are cheap and available in bulk. If those packets aren't available, rice makes a good replacement. Just keep in mind that when using rice, more is better.

Water

Seventy percent of the human body is comprised of water, and it goes without saying that a lack of water puts you in a *piss poor* situation. Even the most naïve person understands water's importance to sustain life.

Storing water is impractical and unsafe. In addition to its weight and volume, it can be difficult to keep it potable over extended periods. Having multiple methods to purify water, on the other hand, is far more practical. Unless your BOL is in Death Valley or some other extremely arid locale, there should be a supply of groundwater available.

Our first basic item, fire, can be used to purify water, so most preppers don't dedicate valuable container space to cases of bottled water. Boiling, as well as manually operated pumps, electronic water filters, and water purification chemicals are all valid processes for making groundwater drinkable and safe.

Keep in mind the electronic option may be the fastest and may purify the highest volume of water, but it will require extra care when buried in the ground. A good idea for these small electronics is a container inside your container, such as a smaller PVC pipe. Also, remember to add a moisture absorber to protect it inside the container.

Manual pumps are the easiest to store. Metal pieces risk corrosion and rust but are an easy fix with a brush and some CLP. Drops and tablets work well, but they aren't perfect and will do little to enhance the taste of muddy water. They're compact and resistant to moisture, especially the drops delivered in glass bottles.

There are straws, filters, wands, and almost as many ways to purify water as there are there are to start a fire.

If your location demands that you store water, then we highly recommend including a purification solution as well. There's no way to be certain that those clear, sparkling bottles of water you buried 10 years ago will be drinkable when exhumed.

Food

Animals provide great examples to emulate when planning to survive during a crisis situation. Territorial, fearful, careful of others, instinctual - the list goes on. Several different animals cache food away. They do it for the exact same reason we do - in case of a future shortage.

What is the best food for long-term storage? MREs (*Meals Ready to Eat*) are great, but they do have a shelf life, contrary to popular belief. Unfortunately, trying to determine the expiration is difficult. The most conservative chart I've seen says an MRE can last 36 months in 60-degree temperature. I will tell you though, I've eaten MREs out of boxes with the production date being five and six years past, and they tasted fine. Still, I wouldn't eat cheese and fruits that are several years old. Use common sense.

MREs are a popular option because they are waterproofed and have silica gel packets already inside. They are also available and affordable; plus they don't taste terrible. But if you have a more sensitive palate, there are other possibilities. The civilian market has a ton of options out there for long-term food. Some of these products have a shelf life of 25 years and come prepackaged perfect for storage. These are packed much the same as their military cousins, with protection both inside and out. While you will not find them served in a four-star restaurant, some folks claim they taste better than MREs.

Many different examples of long lasting food are already in your cupboard. Rice, canned goods, honey, and sugar can all last for years if properly stored. Canned goods are especially good at lasting for years and years. These foods are also much more familiar to people and can provide a morale boost in difficult times. Children can be especially picky eaters, so if you have little ones with a favorite taste, by all means, include that option in your stash. We've had to bug out for hurricanes several times, and believe me, the kids are going to be stressed enough as it is.

By far the most popular sources for extended-life food are the numerous prepacked, ready-made options specifically marketed to preppers. From camp food to our much-touted chocolate nutrition drinks, a wide variety of freeze-dried, dehydrated, or vacuum-sealed options are readily available.

In my own personal experience, dehydrated fruits and veggies taste the best. Many can be eaten straight from the container and have a consistency similar to popcorn.

When it comes to pre-seasoned foods like baked beans or soups, canned goods are always my family's favorite. For breakfast, many of the camping food suppliers have nailed it.

Shelf life and compactness vary by product and preservation method. Prepper foods can be expensive, so be a savvy shopper. For pure emergency ratios in extremely tight spaces, a box of gelatin is an excellent source of compact calories. There's not much nutrition there, but it will keep you going for a bit.

Wrapping canned goods in a layer of duct tape can prevent corrosion. The metal isn't likely to rust, but you can never be too safe.

When it comes to honey, over time it will become somewhat solid, and tends to look unappealing. Heating thickened honey will revert it back to its natural, gooey state. According to news reports, archeologists have removed honey from Egyptian tombs that were thousands of years old. It was still consumable.

For any foods that do not already come in an airtight container the best way to store them is vacuum sealing. Vacuum sealers won't break the bank, but they aren't cheap either. Rice, sugar, dried beans, and dried fruits can be stored with vacuumed sealing. In reality, any dry good can be stored in vacuum-sealed bags for a long time. In addition, you can package other cache items, such as clothing and ammunition.

Air is humid, and we'll reiterate yet again – moisture is not your cache's friend.

If a vacuum system isn't in your financial cards, Mylar bags are cheap, and an airtight seal can help protect carefully selected contents for years. Press as much air out of the contents as possible.

A great calorie and protein fueled food that comes ready to store is peanuts. Planters Dry Roasted peanuts in vacuum-sealed glass containers may be a little plain but have great nutritional value.

CHAPTER 7

MUMMY GUNS

A gun is often a useful tool in survival situations, hunting and self-defense considered primary needs by many preppers.

Beyond these obvious uses, some folks want to store an off-site cache of weaponry just in case things get a little out of hand with gun-control legislation. Should our own government become tyrannical or if our homeland is invaded, many people would see no other choice but to hide their weapons.

It is up to the individual to judge whether the benefits of caching weapons outweigh the risk, inconvenience, and hassle.

Of all the individual items we can stash, weapons are probably the most expensive. For the price of a modest weapon and a few hundred rounds, you could purchase a lot of food, clothing, or other supplies instead. Covering one of your blasters with shovels full of dirt can be a difficult act.

A cached gun is also something to be incredibly careful with. Should someone find your cache, you've now armed what could be a potential predator. Should your cache 'wash up,' you may be arming a naïve child. Most law enforcement would probably just shake their heads at the discovery of food and fire starting gear, but unearthing firearms would be a far more serious matter.

One way to avoid arming the dishonest would be the removal of key components, like the firing pin or the barrel of a pistol. I would either utilize a separate cache for these parts, or since they're small, keep them close at hand. I would also store little to zero ammo with the gun, and keep a separate buried stash nearby. If someone absconds with your deactivated gun, they're still out the ammo and working parts.

When it comes to storing ammo, in general, I wouldn't suggest putting all your eggs in one basket. Separate, small caches require more work but also mitigate risk. As preppers, we take risk seriously, so don't be lazy about your ammo caches. One method might be to store a box of different calibers in a single stash, and then have multiple, smaller stores. The good news is that you can store an amazing amount of pain pills in a very small container. That translates into less digging per site.

Another common sense tip for caching rounds is to put the individual cartridges into magazines in order to conserve space. Popular mags, such as for an AK or AR platform, may be a barter item in a post-event society. Many surplus stores sell used GI models for a few dollars each. You never know.

Even if you don't have the spare mags, take the ammo out of the boxes and place it in a Mylar bag.

Storing guns and ammo is a unique challenge. Detailed preparations are critical as you can clean some rust off of a weapon, but corroded ammo is useless. Utilizing the proper storage materials will go a long way in having a successful weapons cache.

PRESERVATION OF YOUR ARMS

The first step is determining what preservation options are available. Please read this section completely and carefully before attempting any or all of the methods below.

Regardless of the "encasing" option you choose, the first priority is to thoroughly clean your weapons before applying any sort of preservatives. The residue left from modern smokeless powders can retain moisture and may include corrosive chemical components. Over several years, these may inflict significant damage to the weapon. Do your best cleaning routine and be thorough.

No matter which of the methods below you choose, an application of the coating/preservative will be necessary. Do this as quickly as possible after cleaning the firearm and letting it dry, of course.

Some preppers have a saying, "The day you *have* to bury your guns is the day you *should* be digging them up."

COSMOLINE

No discussion of storing firearms would be complete without an introduction to my friend, cosmoline. Now that the pleasantries are out of the way, I'm sure some of you surplus collectors recognize the term. Cosmoline a protective coating that lasts for years and prevents moisture-related defects on your weapons, especially the real good stuff: Mil-Spec Metal Preservative Compound.

For long-term, decade or more storage, there's no better option that I'm aware of.

A lot of readers have probably felt the slow pain of cleaning it off a Mosin or other older, properly preserved, weapon. Cosmoline is a compound used by the military for long-term storage and to transport weapons through hundreds of miles and differing environments. While cosmoline is hard both to apply and remove, that downside is offset by the excellent quality of protection it offers.

The original product was a Vaseline-style substance, perfect for long-term storage. Cosmoline can be applied to wood, metals, and plastics. As a surplus collector, I've cleaned cosmoline off all three of these surfaces and have never seen any adverse effects. While there's no way of knowing how long these weapons had been coated, it wouldn't be unreasonable to assume it was decades.

There are other cosmoline-based products available as well. However my experience has mainly been with the military issued substance. Cosmoline is available and easy to find online, and it is very affordable. A website I trust, offering great customer service and fair prices is *cosmolinedirect.com.*

When cleaning and handling, I personally wear gloves to avoid leaving fingerprints. Fingerprints are comprised of mostly water, and water plus metal is what we are avoiding. Clean the weapons thoroughly, being especially observant of rust. Use an ammonia-free cleaning agent like Hoppe's Elite Gun Cleaner and Copper Terminator. Copper attracts moisture, which is our enemy.

Modern cosmoline is thinner and easier to apply, requiring no heating to use. If you get your hands on some of the older product, it helps to warm it up by submerging the can in hot water. It is most commonly applied with a brush, and this is an effective, but slow method. My preference for applying "thick" cosmoline is via a hand pump sprayer, like one used in gardens for pesticides. This is a quicker method that really helps you get the smaller corners and parts effectively covered.

Cosmoline does not necessarily dry; it thickens on your weapon and leaves a greasy residue behind. This is the protective layer. Wrapping the weapon in a blanket or gun sock is another protective measure to keep dirt and small debris from sticking to the grease.

Cosmoline can be used for wood stocks as I mentioned earlier, but can be difficult to remove. If you desire a more convenient way to preserve your wood, you can use a gun stock wax. Birchwood Casey makes a great one.

After applying a proper coating, wrap the weapon in a heavy plastic, like a trash bag. This will keep any small debris and dirt off the weapon. Prior to wrapping, throw some oxygen/moisture absorbers in; another layer of protection never hurt anything. Then seal this bundle with duct tape.

VACUUM SEALING

A more modern and expensive way to protect your gun is with modern vacuum seal bags designed for guns. I found these online originally, but recently spotted them in a local gun store. Obviously, the idea of long-term storage is becoming more popular.

The brand I have noticed is called ZCorr Vacuum Seal Storage Bags, and it is available from Brownells' online site. These bags are available in handgun, hunting rifle/shotgun and tactical variants. They will not harm optics, non-metal surfaces, and finishes. They have a vapor phase corrosion inhibitor, or VPCI, that protects your firearms for more than twenty years. The bags are tough and tear resistant, and flexible to ease fitting in difficult areas.

They require no special equipment to use. In fact, they're sealed by a normal household vacuum cleaner. The U.S. Marine Corps even uses these bags for long-term storage. The ease of use and dependability make them perfect for a cache, especially when it comes to the burial of weapons.

Other items to seal your firearms include wax paper, Mylar bags, heavy-duty or thick trash bags, barrier paper, or any other similar, robust defense. This type of protection will help maintain any chemical layer on the firearm, instead of having it rub off onto other items in your cache. You can get all of these examples on Amazon and Walmart.

A company called Sorbent Systems has a website where you can order both Mylar bags and desiccants. Also, when vacuum sealing certain parts, some plastics break down faster, especially if there's something in the preservatives that speeds up the process. This is where Mylar can come in handy as a bag-within-a-bag option.

The simplicity and ease of use make bags ideal. I listed cosmoline as the first option simply due to its wide availability and proven track record. When choosing the method best for your situation, it's going to be up to your budget and what's available. The bags are easy to use, but for the cost of two of them, you can cosmoline an entire arsenal. The bags are also harder to find, and in times of an impending natural disaster, they could become scarce.

For my own personal stashes, I use vacuum bags for travel caches where I may need a weapon quickly, without any cleaning or reassembly required.

For long term, redundant storage, I'm "sticking" with chemical preservatives and mummifying the weapon in a light plastic.

COSMOLINE ALTERNATIVES

If time is short, and you have neither cosmoline nor vacuum bags, you may have to look at options on hand. Every gun owner should have some sort of CLP (Clean, lubricate, protect) product. CLP is widely available and very cheap. From sporting goods stores to Walmart, you can find this stuff anywhere. You will also need blankets, sheets, or any kind of cloth material on hand.

Here is an incredibly simple way to quickly store a firearm. Take a spray bottle with CLP and soak a sheet. Wrap the metal parts of your gun in the fabric. The extra plastic or wood parts should be stored separately. This is not a preferred method but should provide you with months, perhaps years of secured storage.

There's USGI grease, which you can consider if your weapons cache is going to be very long-term (multiple decades or more). This thick substance usually comes in small, yellow pots. A great source is eBay. Or, you can purchase Remington's Rem Oil or Tru-Oil from Birchwood Casey. Those are likely available your local gun shop, sporting goods store, or Walmart.

Substances like WD-40 also work in a pinch. Spray them on a rag and rub onto the metal.

You can also make your own cosmoline alternative, which can be easier to remove and apply than the real thing. You can use Coleman fuel or a small amount of white gas. Then add general purpose or wheel-bearing grease, such as the brand Castrol. Some alternative ingredients include paraffin, Vaseline, and other clones. This is useful if you already have these supplies on hand. Mix the small amount of fuel, white gas, or selected substance with the grease until you have a consistency similar to pancake syrup. White gas is recommended over fuel since it makes the grease easier to apply. You don't need much. Do *not* heat during application or removal – **these alternatives are flammable**. If you *do* use authentic cosmoline and a heating method, **do not let it reach 300 degrees** (149.889 Celsius). If you make your own cosmoline, you'll have to find a compatible removal substance for cleaning after you retrieve your weapon.

NOTES ON APPLICATION

If you're unsure how your preservative will interact with your favorite blaster's plastic furniture, remove it and other accessories. Many preppers believe in stripping weapons of plastic and wood parts before applying the protective coatings listed above. The concern is that these substances are designed for metal, and plastic may degrade over the years. Vacuum seal, or wrap the removed items in Mylar to prevent run-off chemical damage.

Coat all metal components thoroughly, paying special attention to areas like contact surfaces. Some of these areas include but aren't limited to slides, actions, and extractors. Coating the insides of hard to reach places, like the inside of the barrel, is important. You can use a long strip of an old rag and run it through the barrel a couple times. When applying preservatives, also pay attention to areas like double tubes.

If you purchase a weapon pre-greased or pre-preserved, do a thorough checkup before caching.

WEAPONS RETRIEVAL

You need to have the supplies on hand when you retrieve your cache and clean your weapons. I recommend packing the cleaners, as well as any required reassembly tools, in the weapons cache itself.

After retrieving your weapon, it's time to remove the cosmoline. Doing this can be a pain, simply because you have to get into every nook and cranny of the weapon, which means completely stripping the piece. Heat works pretty well, but will probably be unavailable in a bug out situation. Mineral spirits, also known as paint thinner, works just as well but can leave a residue. Carburetor cleaner works well, as does lacquer thinner. In my cache, I store a properly protected can of WD-40 with my cache anyway, just in case I have rust issues. Carburetor spray and lacquer thinner are great strippers as well.

Some other degreasers to consider include lighter fluid (again, flammable – do not use this if you made a homemade cleaner or used a flammable alternative) and any solvent. Amazon has lists of solvents specifically for firearms degreasing. Browse your local sporting goods and gun shops for the best fit for your preservative.

Of course, you'll want rags, cleaning rods, patches, brushes, a good workspace, oil to lube the firearm, and maybe an OTIS kit. You probably already have all or some of these. The examples of local shops and sites I've listed so far will have what you need.

SURVIVAL VALUE VERSUS CASH VALUE

Don't misunderstand my intentions in this section. All weapons are worth storing in my opinion, but can you cache all weapons? If you can, good for you. When it comes down to it, you need to consider the weapon's value in a survival situation. Beautiful, gold and silver inlaid over/under skeet guns are great, true works of art, and priced accordingly. Ask yourself, when the shit hits the fan, is that shotgun going to be worth more than an AK or AR15?

Another question you should ask is which gun is more likely to be on the chopping block? Even with the leadership of some anti-gun organizations spouting that their goal is to ban all firearms, your skeet gun will be one of the last they try to take. ARs, AKs, FALs, even M1 Carbines, will most likely be the first to face restrictions or be outlawed.

Keep in mind, the survival value of weapons is more important than cash value. As hard as it may be to part with, that crusty Romanian AK is the way to go. No offense to that beautiful shotgun, though.

CHAPTER 8

AMERICA'S RIFLE AND THE GOAT HORN

"Which weapons should you bury?" you ask. Any. While the choice depends on your individual wants and needs, the possibilities are nearly limitless. Tactical and surplus weapons are good choices, which we'll explore below. For the prepper on a budget or who is uncomfortable shoveling dirt onto a hefty pile of $100 bills, there are choices such as the SKS or Mosin Nagant.

Take a budget-step above those, and you will find selections such as the Romanian WASRs and Russian Saigas as alternatives. For surplus handguns, first generation Glock pistols and S&W revolvers work well. But those are just examples. Do not bury weapons that you rely on and use regularly for your home battery and concealed-carry protection, unless you double-buy a favorite model. At the same time, do not bury weapons that you hardly use or aren't as familiar with as your favorite weapons. They won't be as useful for that crucial moment when you need your cache.

Two of the most prevalent, modern tactical rifles are the AR 15 and AK 47 clones. These weapons are incredibly popular among shooters, and well suited for a variety of roles in a survival situation. I'm not here to argue which is better but to argue they are both great choices.

The popularity of these rifles makes ammunition common, plentiful and affordable. In a SHTF situation, the cartridges for these rifles should be easier to acquire than less popular calibers. These weapons are powerful enough for small to medium game and self-defense.

As of this writing, I can find used, base-model AR15s for around $500. That's a lot of sawbucks to be sticking into a hole and covering with dirt. Yet, I know this weapon. I have spares, cleaning supplies, magazines, furniture, and most importantly, it's my first choice as a prepper/survival weapon. It's what I train with, and that can make all the difference in the world during a gunfight.

Something else that can't be ignored is the compactness factor of these models. As pointed out above, while the height of an AR is just over 8 inches, the upper can easily be separated from the lower and that shortens the length considerably. Compact weapons are going to be easier to cache. A smaller container means less digging, which may not be such a big deal when you're entombing your stash. It can, however, impact the amount of time needed to retrieve your piece. You might be in a big hurry to get out of Dodge. Even if you're all set on a larger container, a smaller blaster will leave room for other items.

Base model, non-US manufactured shotguns are far less expensive. At a recent gun show, I had my choice of pump scatterguns for under $200. I can't speak for the quality/reliability of these weapons, but they are available. Even a new, American made, household name unit can be had for $300 - $350 if you shop around.

The AK family of battle rifles is another prepper favorite, with paratrooper models (folding stocks) commonly available. Again, the wallet-kinetics are going to run in the $450 - $500 range for a used, quality piece. The AK's magazines are a bit bulkier and heavier than the AR 15 magazines.

There are literally thousands and thousands of firearm options, including .22 caliber rifles that disassemble in seconds.

In previous chapters, we devoted a significant amount of time to the subject of waterproofing, both the container and individual components such as firearms. Despite all those precautions, I'm more comfortable with the moisture resistance of military-grade weapons. It's like an additional, labor-free protective layer.

An excellent weapon worth storing is the Mosin Nagant. As a combat weapon, it does have some disadvantages – being heavy, long, and a bolt action. The Mosin makes a great hunting rifle; it's accurate, powerful, and reliable and doesn't require much maintenance. The round it fires is relatively cheap and easy to find on online, as well as being available at most gun stores. Buying a 'spam' can of ammo is a great way to acquire bullets in bulk, and it comes sealed in a waterproof container.

Best part of the Mosin? Its price. Spending $150 dollars would be considered expensive for one of these beasts. A situation may arise where you cannot reach your caches immediately. Buying a couple of these allows a good emergency rifle to be placed in alternate locations for a very affordable investment.

Another weapon I cannot stress enough is some form of .22 long rifle, whether you choose a Ruger 10/22 dressed to the nines or a cheap, surplus, bolt-action Romanian training rifle. The importance of a rimfire in your post-collapse arsenal shows excellent forethought. The ammunition is the cheapest, most common you can find. A box of 550 rounds costs about the same as 50 rounds of 5.56 NATO and is small enough to be carried in a cargo pocket. The round has its limitations and leaves something to be desired in the self-defense category. While it is a small game hunter for sure, in a pinch, it's obviously better than throwing a rock.

MORE WEAPONS PRESERVATION TIPS

Store a weapon with the barrel facedown to avoid oil getting into the action. If you store magazines, grease them and the springs very lightly. Be sure to inspect both during your cache checkups.

Never deface the numbers on your firearms. Defacing is illegal, and can lead to your never possessing another firearm again if someone discovers your cache. It is yet another indicator of wrongdoing.

CHAPTER 9

AMMO: BASICALLY GUN BATTERIES

Proper storage of ammunition should never be overlooked, especially when caching underground. Burying cartridges is perfectly safe if executed properly.

The reasons for stashing large quantities of lead go beyond defensive or hunting needs. Many preppers believe that ammo will become a top bartering item if things get really bad, some predicting that it will become the new currency, more valuable than precious metals or cash.

When possible, stash military grade cartridges, but not necessarily military surplus rounds. Several manufacturers offer "new" mil-spec ammo. The logic behind this choice is that it is often difficult to tell the date of manufacture on various boxes of ammunition. Unlike beer, there's no "born on" date. If stored properly, the shelf life of any quality ordnance is significant, but why fill your cache with a perishable item that is already aged?

For the AR platform, you can typically identify mil-spec cartridges via a couple of different features. First, the caliber will be 5.56mm or 5.56 NATO, as opposed to .223 Remington. If your weapon is chambered for both calibers, which is the case for most modern AR varieties, then the 5.56mm will function just fine. If not, then stick with .223 Remington, as there is a slight difference in the two cases.

Secondly, look for the identifying military classification. In the example to the left, you will see M855, which are sometimes called "green tips," due to the bullets being dipped in a green coating. This

is done so shooters in the field can designate between various types of cartridges (tracers versus piercing as an example).

There is no guarantee that the box of pain pills at your local Ammo-r-us is new, or recently manufactured, but the odds are better than purchasing bulk surplus that you know has been sitting on a shelf in some military warehouse for a significant about of time.

If the ammo comes pre-loaded in "stripper clips," then it is likely to be surplus and have some number of years already deducted from its shelf life. Use these rounds for training and stash the new stuff.

One of the primary reasons why I recommend mil-spec ammo is that most armies demand "crimped" primers in their specifications. There's a good reason for this optional feature.

A crimped primer won't misfire as easily, nor is it as likely to blow back out of the pocket and foul the weapon. Keep in mind that these cartridges may be used for belt-fed weapons (extra vibration and stress), and are designed for harsh, battlefield survival. Some experts believe that crimped primers add to a cartridge's moisture resistance.

It may take a little more extra shopping, but you can find mil-spec ammo that is probably fresher from the factory.

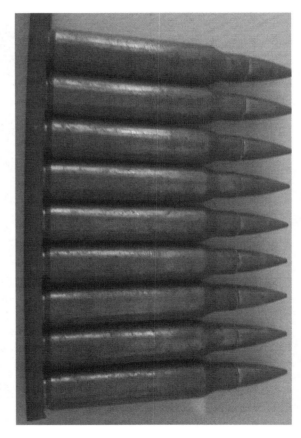

Often I'm asked about "steel case" ammunition, sometimes referred to as "Russian." These cartridges use a steel-type metallic alloy for the case versus the traditional brass. They are typically less expensive, which make them attractive for placing in a hole and covering with dirt.

Urban legends abound concerning steel cased cartridges. I've been told to expect damaged extractors and heard that the powder produces more carbon and thus will foul a weapon after fewer rounds expended. Some folks claim BCG (bolt carrier group) damage, while others say their gas tubes foul quickly. I've fired thousands and thousands of these cheapies through various weapons and never experienced any serious issues. Others will strongly disagree with that statement.

Regardless of what's true or false about cartridges, I can confirm four attributes of steel cased ammo that I have experienced firsthand:

1. It is not as accurate. Some time ago, I was doing research for a magazine article that involved pulling the bullets from new cartridges and then weighing the powder on a digital scale. We tested at least 20 different brands/manufacturers and found that the inexpensive steel ammo had the widest inconsistencies in powder charge and bullet weight. While this has nothing to do with the actual case material, it is an indicator that you get what you pay for.

2. A steel casing doesn't allow for "crimping," as it is not as flexible as brass. This translates into factories having to seal their product with a lacquer rather than pressure molding. Examine the primer, and you'll see a red ring around the pocket. That's a sealant, and when you fire these cartridges, some of that substance finds its way into your weapon's action. While I've never had it cause a malfunction or jam, it can be a bit of extra effort to clean from the firing pin, extractor, and bolt. It's not difficult to imagine long-term buildup would cause issues.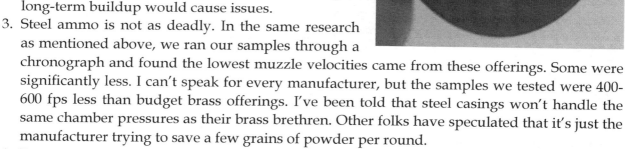

3. Steel ammo is not as deadly. In the same research as mentioned above, we ran our samples through a chronograph and found the lowest muzzle velocities came from these offerings. Some were significantly less. I can't speak for every manufacturer, but the samples we tested were 400-600 fps less than budget brass offerings. I've been told that steel casings won't handle the same chamber pressures as their brass brethren. Other folks have speculated that it's just the manufacturer trying to save a few grains of powder per round.

4. Brass casings are far more corrosion resistant than steel casings. I make this statement based on experience, not as a metallurgist. Where I do most of my training, we do our best to police the area for spent cartridges. Despite a diligent effort, we always miss a few. During these scavenging efforts, you always come across older casings lying in the grass. You can spot the Russian units after a while because they turn the dark red from rust. Brass will tarnish, but after a few hours in a tumbler, they are still very usable for reloading.

If your budget only allows for caching steel ammo, then by all means, use the same steps outlined herein and then dump it in the hole. If the choice is shooting Russian versus brandishing your fist and hurling insults, the choice is easy.

As of this writing, there's really not a huge cost savings associated with buying a lower quality of ammo. The difference is less than $100 per 1,000 rounds of 5.56 NATO. That, however, hasn't always been true. Back in 2012, when shortages of ammunition were common, Russian was significantly less expensive. As with so many things associated with prepping, only you can determine what works best given individual circumstances.

Throughout this guide, we've preached waterproofing, and that's going to continue. Obviously, wet ammo is not good ammo; instead of a bang you're bound to get a puff. Since bulk ammunition can be loosely "molded" to fit the interior of your container, I like threaded PVC the best for storing cartridges.

Silica gel packets or some other absorption material is going to be necessary. In a later chapter, I'll go in depth on using these inexpensive little bags of humidity fighters. Oxygen absorbers, or the other hand, are completely unnecessary for cartridges. Storing ammo is about keeping it dry. External waterproofing is critical, and internal moisture absorption is never a bad idea. After waterproofing the container, filling common, zip-seal sandwich bags with ammunition and then throwing in a couple of silica gel packets inside is adequate.

I am against the idea of oiling your ammo. While CLP puts the 'P' in protect, it's made for guns, not beans or bullets. CLP and Rem Oil are both liquid materials; when liquid meets gunpowder, you may develop some problems. I have had a personal experience with the combination of lubricants and ammo.

I was instructing Marines at a machine gun range when a young Marine showed the classic combination of good initiative and poor judgment. The young man sprayed a good deal of LSA (Lubricant, Small Arms) on his ammunition – something he must have heard in a movie or read in a pulp novel. It was his fourth consecutive misfire before we figured out his issue. His ammo was drenched in LSA, and it had reached the powder.

This cannot only render your ammo unusable but can attract a variety of small debris. These flecks of dirt, carbon, and other foreign objects can add up, causing failures in your weapon and fouling magazines. Plus, trying to load lubricated rounds into magazines could be a pain, rounds slipping and sliding everywhere like little, greased pigs.

I've also noticed an extended muzzle flash when oil/lube gets into the chamber. I can't imagine slicked-up cartridges helping negate this effect. Hands covered in lubrication can hamper your ability to handle that blaster. Ammunition and any kind of lubricant or liquid protecting agent is a bad idea. It's that simple.

Burying ammunition already loaded in magazines isn't a bad idea though. This saves room in your container. A popular urban myth regarding magazines is that a leaving them loaded for an extended period of time will wear them out. This is a complete and total myth. A compressed spring will not wear out. The act of unloading and loading the pillbox is what causes wear and tear. So top 'em off and keep 'em that way.

Ammunition is an item I'd suggest caching in a way that allows you frequent access. Your likelihood of avoiding a nasty surprise will be greatly reduced if you can occasionally check your stash's health. Look for discoloration of the brass. Any sign of a green "crust" is a sure indicator that moisture is working its way into your container.

Consider caching calibers for weapons you do not own. You don't have to actively look for random calibers to cache, but if you stumble on an exceptionally good deal, you might just pick up a box and hold onto it. This ammunition can obviously be handy should you find a new rifle in a bug out situation. Stick to the common calibers. You may not have a 20 gauge or a .308, but someone out there does.

SPEAKING OF BATTERIES

Not long ago, I would have hesitated in recommending that anyone include batteries for a long-term cache.

The shelf life of the typical household power cell just wasn't conducive for the average cache's function. Depending on the source, most products were limited to 2-3 years of storage before experiencing a serious decline in available energy.

Batteries also corrode, producing a discharge that might harm other items inside the container.

Recently, however, my opinion has changed.

Rechargeable batteries have become common, and the technology has greatly improved. Shelf life, if stored "empty" can be 5-10 years for quality NiMH (Nickel Metal Hydride) units. Combined with a solar charger, they can provide a prepper an excellent source of long-term power for smaller devices, such as flashlights, cell phones, GPS, or weapon optics.

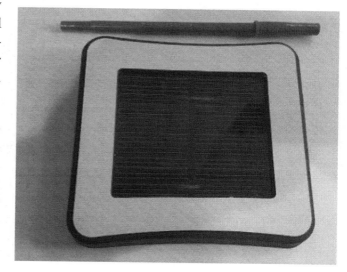

Solar chargers are not as expensive, or as large as you might think. Recently, I purchased the pictured unit at one of those "everything's a dollar," stores, and have been quite impressed with its performance. It will recharge my cell phone in a single day, and while that may not sound like a huge power plant, in a survival situation, accessing a smartphone's GPS or a stored ebook on local plants just might save your bacon.

There are also solar chargers designed for outdoor uses, such as camping and hiking. In my fictional book series *Holding Their Own*, the protagonist uses a folding charger based off of the Goal Zero model I have in my bugout bag. These units can get a little pricy, but having electricity when the grid is down can solve so many survival issues.

One inexpensive option is available for a few dollars at more home improvement stores. Solar landscaping lights come in all sizes and shapes. I know a few preppers who have a package of these little

units to provide indoor lighting in the event of blizzard, tornado, or hurricane. Most of these products have a rechargeable battery inside.

Another new product is from the company Energizer. Their **ECOADVANCED** batteries claim to have a shelf life of 12 years. Now, we're talking a usable item for a cache.

Regardless of what kind, size, of chemistry of battery you plan to cache, how you package the unit is important.

Years ago, while in the field, I experienced a failure that taught me a valuable lesson. My weapon's optic used small "coin cell" batteries. I always stored a few spares in the blaster's pistol grip.

Sure enough, my halo-dot went dead at just the wrong time. "No problem," I thought. "I am prepared!" When I replaced the battery, the optic was still dead. The redundant spare provided no joy.

It was extremely frustrating. I knew both of those cells were new, having been cycled just a few weeks prior. Later, I learned that that some batteries can be drained by touching each other, or by merely touching their surroundings. Now, I take care to keep all conductive ends separated.

PREPARING BATTERIES

The simplest way to make sure your batteries don't short out is to keep them in the original packing. If that is too bulky or unavailable, then wrapping each cell in common, sandwich "cling wrap" has worked well for me. Just make sure to keep each unit separated by a layer of cellophane.

Most solar chargers require a cord and some sort of cradle for the batteries and can only refill one or two different size cells. The careful prepper takes an inventory of all his/her DC powered gear, including flashlights, weapon optics, aiming lasers, night vision, and even tablet computers.

Once you have a list of all the different battery sizes that will be required, you can go about securing the proper charging cradles and spare cells.

CHAPTER 10

FIGHTING THE WAR ON WATER

Waterproofing is probably the second most important thing you can do for your cache; the first, of course, is remembering where you buried your goodies. A buried cache is hidden from most of the elements of the outside world, but moisture is one that will be a constant battle. Soil tends to absorb and retain water, and if it gets through your multiple barriers, the cache may be worthless when retrieved.

Sealing a PVC container is the easiest of the homemade vessels we have listed. This is probably why it appears most often in articles, forum threads, and blogs. A pipe with one threaded end, a screw-on cap, a regular cap, and a dab of plumbers cement and you're good to go. I would love to say it's not that simple, but it really is. Proper application of the cement is the key; most cement is colored blue so you can tell your pipe is sufficiently covered.

The only issue with the above configuration is the threaded parts. For small diameter caches, finding off the shelf pipe that is pre-threaded isn't difficult. My local home improvement stores have shelves of the stuff in practically every size and shape.

If you require a larger diameter, anything over 4 inches, the number of outlets/options diminishes quickly. After one whole day of searching pool supply and landscaping stores, I finally gave up trying to find 8" or larger threaded.

Some weeks later, I was in a mom and pop hardware store, and they had some 10-inch fittings that were threaded. I bought them despite the fact that I had no pipe or "tube." After bringing them home and ex-

perimenting a bit, I lost confidence in the threads' ability to remain waterproof after more than a few open/close cycles. Perhaps that was result was simply a result of my small sampling.

If your intent is only to seal and open your cache once, then by all means, cement both ends with caps, and test the integrity. Submerge in a bathtub and make sure no bubbles come out, and then start digging. Later, after retrieval, your only option is to saw through the pipe and pull out the contents. The vessel is usable only one time.

An alternative to using PVC caps is utilizing a test plug and a knockout inspection cap. These are used by plumbers and irrigation installers to test for leaks after installations and repairs. A test plug is a plastic cap with a rubber seal that utilizes a wingnut to tighten it inside the pipe (pictured).

A knockout cap leaves an alternative entry point if you can't get the test plug out for whatever reason. Seal the knockout cap on the pipe with waterproof silicone sealant. The knockout cap gets its name from the fact you can break it out using a hammer, or even a heavy stick or rock. Perfect to make a back door if your test plug fails.

Test plugs and knock out caps are cheap as well, they cost between four to eight bucks depending on their size. You can find them at any hardware store, from the small mom and pops to the national outlets. Again, finding the larger sizes could be an issue.

Military steel ammo cans do require a little more waterproofing. These cans are very water resistant, but will not last forever with continued exposure to moisture. The main problem with these cans is the lack of any seal. There are ways to handle this issue.

First off, a very easy and very efficient way to seal your ammo can is a waterproof silicone sealant. Loctite waterproof sealant, available for $9.99 is a perfect solution to this problem. Simply apply a line around the lid of the ammo can and allow it to dry. This silicone is similar to what is used in building aquariums.

In case you're already in a bad situation and you find yourself needing a hasty cache, take a look around your garage. A short-term sealant can be made out of various materials. For example, something as simple as duct tape wrapped around the top and sides of the lid and can is an effective short-term seal. A liberal application of caulk can form a temporary barrier.

Another ridiculously simple way to waterproof something is simply wrapping a tarp around the can, or a few heavy-duty trash bags. Heavy layers of spray paint, especially marine grade, can form a good seal over the thin open space on an ammo can. Resourcefulness is the key here, keeping an open mind with what you already have and repurposing it.

The downside to most of these solutions is that once you open the vessel, the seal is broken and must be reapplied to ensure waterproofing. A wise idea would be to cache some additional kind of sealant inside the box with your supplies. A few tubes of Loctite would easily fit without taking up excessive room.

Using heavy, wooden containers for caching presents a challenge, but that can be overcome with a little work. The first step is to apply a layer of waterproof finish. You have to apply some kind of coating on the wood to prevent rotting, warping, and cracking.

A strong varnish is the best. Wooden boats are a hobby for many, and these require a strong, long lasting varnish. Perfection Plus, sold on *yachtpaint.com*, is a good product. It's important to remember these are strong chemicals and to take every precaution when applying them.

Any wood varnish is effective, such as Behr. Some are much easier to apply and far safer. It's not without its harmful vapors and toxicity but less toxic than Perfection Plus. These products are much easier to find, available at most home improvement chains.

If the wooden vessel is constructed using multiple planks, a sealant like Loctite will be required to further waterproof the box. Loctite should also be applied around the edges of where the lid lies. Remember when sealing the cover to the box you can't open it without breaking the seal, so pack some extra sealant to reapply the seal. I also always suggest wrapping a tarp or strong plastic material around a wooden box, no matter how many times you've been over it with a paintbrush and goo.

Plastic ammo cans and water bottles are often waterproof from the factory. Choose plastic ammo boxes that have a rubber seal inside that prevents water from reaching your ammo. Water bottles require even less diligence: If they can keep water in, they can keep water out as well.

After you've sealed the outside, you have an important task to perform. It is time to test your sealing skills. Sealing PVC caches is easy and hard to mess up, but it's still critical to test the seal. Testing ammo cans and wooden containers is important to ensure you know the proper technique to seal and that you are using a proper amount of sealant.

As mentioned above, use a bathtub, swimming pool, pond, lake, stream, bucket, or any water source that is deep enough and has a smooth surface. For example, standard ammo boxes can fit fine in a five-gallon bucket.

Look for air bubbles.

VACUUM PACKING

Vacuum sealing, something we've mentioned before, can be incredibly valuable for waterproofing. Smaller containers, especially PVC containers that are only a few feet long, are the perfect size to seal in a vacuum bag before you bury them. Smaller surplus ammo cans, like the 7.62 linked cans, would be easy to vacuum seal.

Vacuum sealers and bags are easy to find. Models like the Foodsaver V2244 are available on Amazon for under a hundred dollars. Cheaper models such as the Seal a Meal VS108 are available for less than $50. Twenty feet of bag material currently costs about $10.

The bags are available in a multitude of different sizes. Eight-inch diameter bags will probably suffice most containers. Bags are available in 11 inches as well. Most of these replacement rolls allow you to taper the length of the bag to your individual needs, so even long containers can be sealed.

MOISTURE ON THE INSIDE

A serious threat to your store is the accumulation of humidity on the inside of your containers. Any packaging, wrap, clothing, can, or plastic item will have some level of moisture on its surface as you place it inside the container. Even the internal air, trapped right before you engage the final seal, will contain water. Wide ranges of temperature swings can result in condensation.

This presents a real threat to the items stored inside. Add to this the possibility that the failure of a single food can, tube of medical crème, or other liquid can decimate your entire inventory. It quickly becomes clear that having some sort of moisture absorption on the inside of the vessel is a worthy preventative step.

The easiest and most efficient and reliable way to fight moisture inside your container is silica gel. Those small packets you find in shoeboxes marked, "Do not eat," are silica gel packets. You have probably noticed them in a variety of packages to prevent moisture from ruining consumer goods. Often, you find that a single, small 1-gram package will protect a pair of shoes in your closet when it takes about 10 of these tiny containers to protect the size of a shoebox for long-term storage.

The best thing is you can find these items for sale at home improvement stores and online retailers like Amazon.com. They are available in bulk and are very affordable. If you utilize these packets, be aware that any accessing of the vessel will require replacing the silica. When you pop the seal, humidity goes rushing in with the fresh air. Many of these packets will change colors from blue to pink indicating they've done their job. This indicator may also point to a small leak in your container.

So how many are you going to need to seal your cache? This is difficult to calculate exactly so what I'm about to suggest errs on the side of caution. Essentially, it takes five grams of silica gel per 1 gallon of space, or approximately 237 cubic inches/.14 of a cubic foot. Always plan on using more than necessary, especially if your measurements aren't exact. Silica gel isn't something that will break the bank, so a little extra isn't going to hurt your pocket.

Another option is pouring your desiccant of choice directly into the container. This can get a little sloppy, so you can make a bag of out some sort of mesh, like cheap, nylon pantyhose or a similar material.

Larger containers of silica are widely available online, as well as in most home improvement stores. Check marine supply outlets and reloading supplies. I've found a 40-gram canister of silica gel for $6.00 at MidwayUSA.com. This canister protects 22 gallons of space or 3 cubic feet. Perfect for large containers, they also change color to indicate it's time to change them. There are also packs of 10 desiccants on Walmart's website, or you can order from Uline.com or Amazon. You can also find homemade recipes online that can be even more cost-effective.

Some of these products are rechargeable as well; The MidwayUSA example can be reused over and over. Simply put the used canister in an oven and bake at 300 degrees for 3 hours.

I mentioned rice as a moisture absorber earlier. Rice will not work nearly as well as silica gel. When using rice to absorb water, you have to appropriate a considerable amount of container space for your rice. Rice does work well in individual containers, like resealable bags. An example would be placing flashlight batteries or ammo in a resealable bag, and then filling any remaining space with rice.

Another source of an efficient moisture absorber at home is kitty litter, Tidy Cats in particular. Tidy Cats already has silica gel in it. The key to this is not allowing your kitty litter to be exposed too often before you turn it into packets. To turn it into packets you can use a variety of materials you can easily find around your house.

The first step is baking the kitty litter. Odd, I know. Similar to recharging the silica gel canister, but it must be done prior to use. Sprinkle it on a cookie sheet and preheat your oven to 250 degrees, then bake it for four hours. This will guarantee it will be nice and dry.

Next, you need to identify your packaging material. A variety of materials can be used. They must allow the silica gel access to the air for absorption purposes, so plastic is out of the question for the most part. Coffee filters are great. Old clothes such as socks and ladies pantyhose can be repurposed successfully.

Take the kitty litter while it's still warm, being careful not to burn yourself, and place it inside whatever packaging material you've chosen. Seal the packaging material – staple the coffee filter closed, tie off the sock, whatever you need to do to seal it. If you are not immediately putting this in your cache, place it in an airtight container, like Tupperware.

If, for whatever reason, you really want to use a plastic packaging container, or maybe that's all you have on hand to store the baked kitty litter, then you need to put holes in it. Utilize a small needle, ice pick, nail, etc. Also after handling silica, wash your hands to be safe. While handling, it is wise to be mindful of any you have dropped. Silica is poisonous, and kids and pets are always at risk of ingesting it.

More desiccants include salt, (though its results are not as good), calcium chloride (very effective), kitty litter (see the tutorial in this section), plasterboard, wallboard, non-dairy creamer powder – anything that absorbs moisture and combats humidity. Liquid nitrogen also works, but it can be expensive. And if you choose to use liquid nitrogen, be careful not to damage its contents. Condensation can build up while using it, making it essentially liquid oxygen (not good). Dry ice will also work, but it requires even more special attention and care than liquid nitrogen. Make sure the ice is completely melted before sealing.

For an air displacer, you can use inert argon gas. You can "fill" your container with the gas. Few people go this route, though, as this option is also expensive.

As a last resort, or if you don't have any access to desiccants or humidity-combating substances, you can remove humidity with a hair dryer. Just give it to the cache for a few minutes. Adding as many items as possible to your caches also decreases humidity levels, since there's less room in the container.

SEALING

The options for sealing your container are as wide and varied as the vessels themselves. This step should be pre-planned so that it can be executed immediately after inserting your desiccant. You can add multiple seals for good measure. While moisture is the enemy, the atmosphere contains water. Press the air out of the bags or sections, and eliminate air pockets when and where you can.

There's Teflon tape, PVC glue, epoxy, rubber cement, or anything else strong and heavy-duty. For example, when using Teflon tape on threaded PVC pipe, wrap around the end cap and make sure to cover all of the threads. Go over them twice, clockwise, so when you screw on the cap, the tape isn't bunched or wrinkled. You can add the PVC cement as well. You can also use a rubber composition gasket with a metal rim.

Whatever you do, make sure your choices are fit for airtight containers and can be removed (or scraped or chipped) without damaging them if you want to reuse the vessel. This is a requirement if you plan to make regular inspections of the cache.

Even if your container already has an airtight seal, additional, yet minimal sealing makes a good backup.

You should also consider inner and outer wrapping materials for the cache. Regardless of where you put your cache, you'll want to give the container even more protection, especially if you choose a container that's less expensive and heavy-duty. Here are some suggestions:

- **Moisture-resistant paper**. That wrapping paper you use in your kitchen for leftovers? That works well. Again, also widely available, inexpensive, and you probably already have some. It can provide long-lasting protection, even on its own, and can prevent substances (cosmoline, wax, grease) from contaminating other items in the container.
- **Rubber repair gum**. This is used on tire repairs, so it's widely available. Check auto supply shops, mass retailers like Walmart, or Google search. It's self-sealing and can be used as an outer wrapping, in addition to what you're already using. Repair gum comes in several different densities. The downside is that the gum can rub off on other items in the cache, so plan to use inner wrapping materials. Depending on your container, choose the highest level of thickness when purchasing, like two millimeters. For watertight sealing, apply gum, then apply pressure to bind the two rubber surfaces together. You'll have a seal around half an inch wide. Make sure the backing stays on the rubber bond, so it doesn't stick to items.
- **Grade C barrier material**. This cloth contains microcrystalline wax used for long-term storage or overseas shipments and is self-sealing. It can be applied like Teflon tape. Try shipping supply companies that carry papers stored to government specifications. The downside is the material can be easily broken by pests. This substance has a low melting point. It can be used as inner wrapping over items.
- **Wax**. The microcrystalline is also available as a wax on its own. It's available through packaging and shipping supply retailers, and you can find the Renaissance Wax brand online on Etsy and eBay. You can also use similar waxy substances, such as paraffin, as I mentioned earlier.

Once you're all done, it's time to test the seal. If you're storing underwater or in a high humidity/moisture area, then you'll want to test your cache. Simply make sure the container is air and watertight, then submerge in water. Watch for bubbles escaping the container. If possible, try to use hot water, since the temperature can bring out leaks or defects that otherwise wouldn't be revealed in cooler temperatures.

SUMMARY

So far, we've reviewed the basics of building a cache. We've highlighted the importance of proper selection of containers, waterproofing inside and out, storing guns, and a small list of necessities. Every cache is going to be different, and we can't advise a universal cache for everyone. We wanted to leave you with some ideas and some things to keep in mind. It's important to stay flexible and think outside the box. Stay resourceful; pay attention to what is already around you. Cache success is all about adaption, resourcefulness, and caution.

CHAPTER 11

STASH THE CACHE

We have established that our cache is best hidden underground. So what goes into digging a hole? Seems like a kind of idiot-proof idea, with the popular perception of ditch diggers being uneducated. Well, the act of digging a hole is easy, but quite a few factors need to be considered before breaking ground.

DISADVANTAGES OF BURIAL

First, it can be difficult to locate your cache once you've hidden it. Retrieval can also be inconvenient, due to the high amount of labor involved. You also need high-quality supplies for burial, conceal-ment, and protection.

There is a lot of advance planning and consideration before the stash is constructed – including re-covery, maintenance checks, and verifying that the cache is still there for your peace of mind.

You also have to consider scheduling and rescheduling due to weather, emergencies, etc. You must be vigilant.

Some time ago, I set aside a Saturday to go check my vault. A sudden family commitment caused me to reschedule.

The following weekend was already booked, so I pushed it out. Again and again, something came up that delayed my visit. After a while, it simply slipped my mind for several months. A segment from a television news show reminded me.

It was a good thing I hadn't waited much longer.

My BOL location had experienced record rainfall at that time. That, and the fact that the earth had settled around my container had led to perfectly circular mini-lake right over the top of my precious stash.

While the chances of someone seeing that standing puddle of water weren't high, if a hunter or hiker did walk by they would probably be scratching their head in wonderment. Curiosity can kill a cat and a cache.

However, for maximum protection, going subterranean should be at the top of your list. Unless a suitable location is beyond your circumstances, creating a tomb is by far the best option.

WHERE NOT TO DIG

So you have your container stocked, properly prepped and waterproofed. Now you move on to the idea of actually digging and burying your cache. In addition to the investment of time and labor in the prep, your stores might be expensive or irreplaceable. The selection of a site is critical.

The first piece of advice I can give you is never bury caches on private property that's not yours. Doing so could open you and the property owner to a series of problems no one wants or needs. First, you can face a trespassing charge. Second, if you get caught burying a gun and ammo on a stranger's property, imagine the questions you're going to be asked. Third, if a homeowner finds this cache on his property, it's almost certain the contents won't belong to you anymore. Things could get ugly, which typically draws the attention of the authorities.

In addition to all of the above, ethics questions can come into play. Consider a situation where new gun legislation is passed. Even if the property owner is like-minded, are you willing to let someone else take the blame if your now-banned weapons are found on their property?

"But, Joe," you might counter, "I've known Mr. Smith for years. We're the best of friends. He doesn't mind."

Today he might not mind. No one knows about the future, and quite frankly, I don't trust any relationship to be absolutely foolproof. I've seen siblings split by inheritance fights, long-term marriages fail, and business partners turn on each other like rabid wolves.

Public property is only a slightly better option, in my opinion. You'll most likely be breaking the law if storing any sort of weapons, including an humble pocketknife. Again, our goal is to operate within the letter of the law, try to keep the authorities out of our affairs, and not hand them an excuse to pry open our gun safes. In addition to legal issues, government-owned land often involves the risk of high traffic. Picture yourself parading through the local game preserve with a post-hole digger and a large container – certainly not the best scenario for hiding your treasure.

If you want to test my theory on the government being very interested in your cache, watch what happens when someone observes you burying a PVC pipe and assumes its some kind of explosive. Always be cautious and choose the public land you use wisely. Parks are not a good idea at all. Kids love to dig. Dogs love to dig. And you do not ever want to bury something that a child could find and play with.

Another risk involved with any site, public or private, is game cameras. My bug out location's perimeter is ringed with infrared, motion-detecting lenses. The system emails my computer if any snapshots are recorded. Even if you are using your own property, keep in mind that the authorities may seize your computers and scan through your pictures if they think you're a really bad person. Video evidence of your popping a couple of shovel-handle blisters before dropping that rifle-shaped PVC tube next to the old pine tree is a sure-fire way of having your life invaded by badges and lawyers.

Avoid abandoned buildings. If you've ever visited a civil war battleground or a public beach, you've seen the swarms of locusts descend upon the earth with their metal detectors and spades. I own one. It's a fun activity, and occasionally I find cool stuff.

Those who seriously participate in "treasure hunting" are always looking for areas that experienced either a historical event or high amounts of human traffic. Old schools, abandoned roadside gas stations, crumbling country churches, and similar structures are prime hunting grounds for these folks. It's for this reason that my rally point stash at the church isn't buried.

If you have no choice, about the best example of public land I can think of would be a state forest or nature preserve. This assumes no laws are being broken, of course. These areas are often vast, covering thousands of acres that might offer protection from prying eyes. The sheer size of these reserves reduces the chance of someone else stumbling across your dig site. It is doubtful children will be running around the wilderness unsupervised. It's even less likely they'll be digging anything up.

Your private property is obviously the most preferred area. It is highly doubtful any laws will be in place to restrict your digging. The likelihood of anyone finding your cache is next to none, and if somehow they do, it is trespassing and theft. A weapon's cache in a tyrannical government or foreign invaders scenario present some danger – if it's on your property, it's your ass. Even if your bug out location is a place you don't regularly visit, the fact it is underground makes accidental discovery far less likely.

If you're digging deep, beware of utility lines, sewage pipe, sprinkler plumbing, and other obstructions that may be obstacles, or could even result in injury (electrocution), or an expensive repair. Most rural underground utilities are marked. Most private sewage treatment, water and gas lines are not.

Each location will have its pros and cons, and the choice will ultimately have to be a personal decision. Your burial/concealment site needs to be as easily accessible as possible for emplacement and recovery. Private property may be ideal, but if you live in the city without a yard, that obviously isn't going to happen. Urban areas make it much more difficult to bury anything, so your best option might be an aboveground hiding place as covered in a later chapter.

Now that we've discussed the general areas you can hide your cache, I want to narrow it down some to give you a few ideas on specific locations to utilize and those to avoid. As I said before, it's critical to keep an open mind and think outside the box. The suggestions within this book may not be your ideal answer, but hopefully they make you think. The greatest tool you have in implementing a successful cache is your mind.

Stay away from lowlands, the bottom of a hill or culverts. Anything on the low side of a slope is bad news. The reason why is perfectly clear to anyone who has ever dealt with floods. Obviously, precipitation or liquid will seek the lowest elevation, but have you ever really examined your potential cache sight after a strong rainstorm or snowmelt?

Swamps, marshes, and bogs may be remote and seldom frequented but are still a bad idea.

Look around your area and take note of any gradual slopes, dips, or other undulations. There are probably a few you've never noticed. A normal rainstorm is inconsequential for these slight slopes, but after a flood, the potential effects in these areas will be apparent. The less water that your cache is exposed to the better. Not only that, but digging the cache up underwater is going to be nearly impossible.

Another dig site to avoid is any type of dirt road, logging trail, 4x4 recreational area, or any area where vehicles may regularly pass. Why is this important? Well, your cache is going to open up an area of packed dirt, and your cache basically forms a bubble. The weight of a vehicle driving over your cache can break your container and destroy your inventory.

Roads, in general, are not a safe choice. There are just too many witnesses, and it's a prime spot for construction, phone line maintenance, and more. Remember, it may take hours to bury a large cache and almost as much time to retrieve it. Where are you going to go if headlights appear on the horizon? Rule out this option, period.

It's best to avoid sinking a hole in the vicinity of trees if at all possible. First of all, the roots can make digging exponentially more difficult. Even if you overcome that headache, roots will grow and could potentially crack or bind your container to the point where it allows moisture to ruin your stash.

Another problem with burying items close to trees is that they are occasionally knocked down by storms. If a larger specimen uproots, a tremendous amount of soil can be displaced by the root ball and potentially expose your hoard.

Digging in sand is always an issue, especially loose silt which tends to collapse and can be eroded by water or wind.

Clay is a good, strong material but tends to absorb and hold water longer than other dirt.

Streams, creeks, and gullies should be avoided, even if they appear dry and unused. Most desert dwellers know the danger of flash floods, such events often washing away large sections of surrounding turf.

Mudslides are another potential disaster for caches. Stay away from mountainsides that aren't primarily rock with a thin layer of topsoil.

Avoid areas that are just outside of urban sprawl. My primary residence is suburban, and for 14 years, we've enjoyed a nice, undeveloped woods just behind our home. Last year I awoke to the sound of bulldozers and earth moving equipment roaring down our street. Within two weeks, the bordering forest was gone, building lots were elevated, and drainage pipes were being installed. If I had placed a cache on that property, it would have been lost, or worse yet, discovered.

Ultimately – just use common sense.

WHERE TO DIG

If there were such a thing, I would describe the perfect cache location as follows:

On my property.

- Within walking distance of my home, but not too close.
- On a higher plateau of land, with proven drainage.
- Visible from the residence, but concealed from neighbors or passersby.
- Some landmarks available to record the spot and assist with recovery.
- Some feature to disguise or camouflage the cache.

Sound too good to be true? No, it's not. One of my BOLs has just such a spot.

A pasture lays 100 meters behind the cabin that is clearly visible from inside. It's high and dry, with the nearest stream several hundred meters away. It is surrounded by trees, but there are no roots to deal with in the immediate vicinity. There are, however, two large boulders on a plum line that would make recovery, even in darkness, very simple.

Best of all, there is an excellent deception.

Many rural homes burn or bury their own garbage. Scheduled visits by waste management trucks simply aren't available, so the household production of trash is either stored in a mini-landfill or incinerated – sometimes both.

Add in brush, leaves, fallen trees, and other natural waste of a multi-acre property, and the need for local disposal is multiplied.

At the BOL, we burn our garbage and have since the place has been occupied. A tractor is used to dig a shallow trench, which then receives the household production of food wrappers, paper products, and the occasional appliance gone bad. We incinerate it regularly to keep the odor down and pests away. Every few years when the trench is nearly full, the ashes and remnants are covered, and the process starts all over again.

Why do I consider this the perfect spot for a cache? First of all, few thieves are going to want to dig in a trash pile. Secondly, the amount of scrap metal and debris in the area would make a metal detector's head explode. The catalog of odors might confuse a K-9 searcher or other curious animal. The soil has been previously disturbed, so digging in any area that was used 20 years ago will be a little easier than virgin turf. Lastly, it's an area that is frequently visited, so I can keep an eye on the burial site.

My situation may be simply good fortune, however, some of the criteria for my perfect "spot" can be recreated if they don't already naturally exist in the locations available to you.

Begin by making your own checklist of what you consider the perfect parameters for a hide. Use mine from above while adding or subtracting your own preferences. Always keep detailed notes as you proceed through your analysis.

You can begin scouting certain aspects before ever visiting the physical site. How far away is the nearest running water? Use Google maps and plot the distance. Want to know the topography? How often does the river overflow its banks? Are there any plans to build a new interstate highway or other major construction projects in the area? The internet is your friend, with many real estate, county government and local blogging sites containing a wealth of information. Find the nearest home or property that recently sold and look it up. The disclosures should indicate previous flood damage, elevations, and other sordid details to help you make an informed decision.

After you've exhausted the information available from your computer's monitor, begin visiting the sites in person. Again, keep notes, use your checklist and make a wise decision.

The route to and from a cache site is important if it's any distance from your primary residence or BOL. Does the location require travel by interstate? Are there multiple access points if the primary route is blocked by traffic or the authorities? Can you drive a motor vehicle close to the site? How rugged is the terrain there and back? Remember, you'll be carrying tools in and the contents of your cache out. Multiple trips reduce security, and time may be crucial.

As recommended above, we like multiple cache sites. Don't stop scouting once you find a great spot. Multiple stashes increase security and survivability.

You'll also want to incorporate the availability of reference points into your selection criteria. These are landmarks or waypoints that help you recognize you're on the right track after what may be months or years passing since you last visited the cache.

One of my BOLs is in the desert, and such markers can be critical in a broad, featureless landscape. Thick forests are another venue where these might be useful. You can use natural features, such as an unusual rock formation, lake, or notable hilltop. I would avoid trees and riverbanks as these can change or disappear over time. Manmade features that are semi-permanent can also be utilized. Railroad tracks, bridges, radio towers, or cross-country power lines may help you find your way to that long-ago buried stash.

When it's finally time to scout the physical locations, always try and note the details of how you would initially create the cache and then visit for follow-ups. Natural concealment is important. Come up with solutions to questions such as:

- How can you conceal your footprints to and from the site?
- Where will you park your own vehicle while working on the cache?
- What happens if snow covers reference points or heavy rain-washes parts of the concealment site away?
- If you hide the cache in tall grass, won't someone notice if the grass has been trampled?

When scouting, do a reasonable level of security checks. How many folks live nearby? Are there deer blinds? ATV or 4x4 tracks? What about empty beer bottles? Is the location a favorite place for the local teenagers to party? Are there spent cartridges lying around from target shooters or hunters? Put on your sleuth hat and figure out who, if anyone, is visiting the locale, and why.

Again, avoid spending too much time at the burial site and the routes. At any point, if you need to ask a question of a local, obviously do not reveal your plans. Don't even disclose why you're asking. Posing as a tourist is your best bet if someone tries to pry.

If a good spot exists for you to observe the concealment site, it may be worth a Saturday to simply stay quiet and do a little stakeout work. Since most folks are off work on the weekend, you'll get to see whether or not the well-isolated spots you have in mind are as remote as they seem.

You can't control everything. Pick a site, route, and reference points you'll make the most of, and be able to have maximum control over what happens at your burial site. I can't stress this enough – *use common sense*. Consider the facts.

WHEN TO BURY

If possible, bury at night, without snow on the ground, without rain or high humidity, and not too late in the fall or winter, so the ground isn't frozen. Avoid weekends or digs late in the week when traffic will naturally be heavier. Earlier in the week is best. Sunday and Monday nights tend to be quietest times, according to police logs.

Be aware that nighttime activity requires the use of lights, and that the illumination of your worksite may be visible for a considerable distance. If there's any chance of your torches drawing unwanted attention, work at dawn or dusk.

If you've followed our advice, and your container is pre-sealed, fog is great cover. If not, the humidity is something to avoid if possible. Check moon phases – for example, a full moon provides more light for digging, but offers less security.

Going into the woods during the local hunting season is a bad idea. Plan your cache visits around such periods.

TIPS: RETRIEVAL, CHECKUPS, TEST-RUNS, AND SITE-SCOUTING

Whether you're doing a test-run or just a checkup, find a good spot for your car, bike, horse, or whatever you used to get there. Here are some additional tips to consider when visiting the site:

- While driving to or from the site, wrap your digging equipment and cache components in a tarp or sheet to keep them out of sight from prying eyes. You may get pulled over for a traffic violation or decide to stop for a burger. Nosey people are everywhere.
- Leave your smartphone at home, or at least turn it off before starting out. If you truly want to avoid any cell tower tracking of your location, wrap the phone in aluminum foil. I'm not kidding. This really works. Try it.
- Don't drive a car/truck with a factory installed GPS and one of those "vehicle assistance services." They can track your vehicle's location.
- Pay cash for any and all expenses like gas and food while in the area. Don't use your credit card for anything.
- Try staying within old tire tracks as you arrive/approach.
- Don't make too much noise, like slamming the door or having the radio on.
- If necessary or practical, purchase camouflage netting to cover your car.
- Treat the visit like a hunting trip, implementing noise discipline and wearing clothing that blends in. Take bug spray, water, and other essentials required for a day outdoors.
- Have a cover story in case you bump into a game warden or local citizen. In addition to my digging and measuring tools, I always take my metal detector. It's the perfect excuse for having a shovel and other equipment in case you're observed. Carry a hiking guide or a bird-watching book might offer another good cover. If there's a lake nearby, tote a fishing pole and small tackle box.

DIGGING

So you've chosen a good location and decided you're ready for the dirty deed. Aside from your favorite digging tools, here are a few more things you'll want to bring: Probe rod, hatchet, pickaxe, machete, flashlight, ground sheets for loose dirt and soil, gloves, tarp, cache container and contents, spare weapon where legal, and a helper or helpers if more than one person is involved in your cache circle.

If you don't normally work with your hands, take along **GLOVES**.

Sharpen all of your chosen digging tools – you'll thank me for that later.

Once you know where you're going to dig, it's a relatively simple thing to do. It also sucks. If you're not used to "making a hole," be prepared for spending a lot more time and physical effort than you might imagine. Depending on the soil, time of year, and your arsenal of excavating tools, this simple act can be frustrating and exhausting.

Depth, coupled with a little bit of cleverness is going to play an important role here. Applying a few techniques to dig is going to make all the difference.

Before breaking ground, a few choice things need to be understood about how deep you should go. Beyond the obvious role of putting the cache in the ground, your location can impact several factors. I am originally from Florida. Finding a basement in Florida is like finding a unicorn. The water level underground is pretty high, and you're likely to meet water after only a few feet. So when burying a cache in Florida, I will have to focus on a good waterproof cache, and digging the appropriate depth.

If you live in an area that experiences harsh winters, be aware that the ground can freeze. This can make digging out a deep container a pain in the ass. Imagine if you don't have a shovel. Digging in frozen earth with some makeshift device is going to be a hassle, and you will risk injuring your hands. The not having a shovel situation is a very real possibility in a SHTF situation. So even in the

summer months having to dig with your hands will be a timely act and is bound to cause fatigue. Going too deep can easily lead to regret later.

Another issue with the freeze and thaw cycles involves the surfacing of your cache. I've seen this with my own eyes.

I'm not sure of the physics behind the entire process, but if your location is someplace that regularly sees temperature variations above/below freezing, your cache can get "pushed" to the surface.

Pictured is an example of a small PVC stash buried at least 20 inches below the surface by a relative. In less than three years, after the final spring snow, look what magically appeared from the depths.

This example also provides additional justification for painting your container a dark color.

If your burial site doesn't allow for vertical placement of the cache, consider burying horizontally. This can accommodate for limited space you may encounter, such as on a hill or a bank. However, there's also the possibility of the dirt washing away gradually, leaving the cache exposed.

What are the risks in producing a trench that is too shallow? The most worrisome would be discovery. We consider this the worst possible situation involving a cache. Another consideration is rain either washing the container out or of the damaging effects of exposure to the wetter topsoil after a storm. A third factor is animals. Many creatures are curious and will be able to detect the unusual scents of a cache and decide to check it out. It's unlikely a metal ammo cache will ever be penetrated by an animal, but if something smells good enough, your PVC pipe can become a chew toy.

I believe the optimal choice is to plan for one or two feet of dirt on top. If your container is a foot tall and you're burying it with two feet of cover, you'll be digging three feet, one foot for the container, two feet for the proper amount of dirt. This depth will conceal scents, and not be an overwhelming amount to dig with little to no tools. Consider burying a decoy above the real thing.

Once you've decided the size your excavation is going to be, you should consider what tools are necessary to sink the hole.

The most common would be the household spade or shovel. These tried and true earthmovers are cheap, easy to pack, and jacks of all digging trades. If you're buying one just for this activity, I would recommend a longer handle and aggressive point at the tip of the blade.

Another common, manual tool is a post-hole digger. As the name implies, it is commonly wielded to dig fence postholes. If you're burying a tube-shaped container, this may be your best option. Be warned, operating the two, scissor-like handles uses a unique set of muscles. Around $50 new.

You can also go with power tools, such as a two-man, gas-powered auger. These can be rented at various outlets. They are heavy, in case you've got a long trek to your site. They are also loud and require more than one person to operate, so someone else is going to know the location of your cache.

If you're not going very deep, and you want to approach the site as clandestinely as possible, consider yet another military issued piece of kit, the E-tool. Back in the day, these were called an entrenching tool, but that has now changed according to our US Marine co-author.

An *excavation* tool, also known as an e-tool, is a common device issued to the military. An e-tool is a small folding shovel that usually comes with a case. The cases offered various means of attachment to a pack, including PALS strips and gator clip attachments. The Gerber model currently for sale in most camping stores has a saw blade installed on one side. This toothed blade is incredibly helpful to cut through roots.

If you're digging on your own land that is an active ranch or farm, you're probably already quite familiar with digging holes and probably have more sophisticated equipment at hand than mentioned here.

These little shovels have a little bit of weight to them, and can be used as picks to break up tough dirt. A good model, like the Gerber, is tough and reliable and able to take a beating. The ability for it to fold up makes it easy to pack and requires very little room. It could even be used as a makeshift weapon in a pinch.

Dirty Deed Tips

- If there is a grass or sod ground cover, take a moment to "peel" it back carefully so you can replace it after the cache is buried. This will help disguise the dig site.
- Spread a tarp or large trash bag on the ground next to the intended hole and dump your dirt there. After inserting the container and refilling, you can haul the excess soil away. After you're done digging and burying your cache, you can wrap your tools and avoid telltale dirt that might soil your vehicle. Again, operational security should never be taken lightly.
- You can put the probe rod to further use by surveying the area to get a feel of it or double-check the cache's exact location during retrieval or checkups. When probing for the perfect dig spot, make sure there's a balance between security and ease – for example, while loose soil and loam are easier to dig, they are also easier to be discovered due to metal detectors or erosion.
- Make sure the burial site contains no trace of your presence or your cache. Check your surroundings before, during, and after digging. Listen, look, and smell for any changes in your surroundings as you dig. Leave everything the way it was before you arrived as much as you can. Get rid of footprints, drag marks, etc. Better yet, disturb as little of the site as possible. Dispose of extra soil far away from the actual burial site.
- A good knife can be an effective shovel – not the best choice, but it will save your hands. Marines have used the good, old KA-BAR as knives, hammers, and even digging utensils.
- Strong smelling soaps, like Irish Spring, are a good animal deterrent. The body wash is not the best choice; it will wash away too fast. Using a cheese grater and a brick of soap is a good way to disperse a small amount of solid soap. Eventually, the soap will wash away, and this process will need to be repeated.

CHAPTER 12

ALTERNATIVES TO BURIAL

You might not want to bury, or it's just not an option, especially if your situation doesn't allow for subterranean activity, or your cache consists of, say, gasoline. Consider these choices:

Home Sweet Home

Maintaining a stash in your primary residence can be attractive on so many levels. The supplies and kit are there, right next to you. You're less likely to worry about theft as compared to some remote mound in the woods. It takes less time and trouble to verify your stash is safe and secure.

If your BOL has a structure, like a home or cabin, the advantages decline, but it can still be a workable solution. Like any cache location, there's always a compromise.

There are downsides to consider, too.

I have food, water, ammo, fuel, and a gun safe full of weapons at my home, even though we plan to bug out if an event occurs. Again, I live in hurricane country, so we've packed up the truck and gotten the hell out of Dodge on numerous occasions. In my case, as I'm sure applies to many readers, it doesn't make any sense to have my backup cache at the same location. If the big, bad wolf huff and puffs, I'd lose everything. As stated previously, any number of life events, such as a house fire, could destroy my entire inventory of in-home preps.

Be warned that any in-home cache is most likely going to be discovered by a K-9 unit or a search by the authorities. They will come in numbers and aren't in any hurry, sometimes taking days to completely ransack a home or office. No matter how clever or well concealed, most stashes will be discovered.

While the vast majority of burglars are complete idiots, not all criminals fall into the intellectually challenged mold. Some even surf the internet and look at pictures of in-home secret stashes and disguised furnishings. Any cache is at risk.

If you have a family, it's difficult to imagine a complex, in-home project that wouldn't be observed by children, visitors, or relatives. That translates into people knowing the location of your stash.

If you don't own your own home, any sort of structural modification, such as storing behind walls or digging a basement bunker is out of the question.

In this specific case, you're most likely going to employ covert furniture, or use one of the alternatives listed below. A quick internet search will produce dozens of different options, including entertainment systems that are cleverly disguised gun cabinets, beds with secret storage compartments, and even fake wardrobes. Many of the examples I've seen are do-it-yourself projects, complete with blueprints.

No matter how you plan to hide your hoard, you'll want to follow the preservation and waterproofing techniques as outlined above. Even if your goodies are going to be housed inside a wall, under insulation in the attic or behind a secret mirror, leaks and water damage can occur. Recently, I had an attic mounted water heater fail while we were away for the day. We lost everything in two closets and had to replace entire walls. Oddly enough, at the exact same time, our neighbor had an upstairs pipe pop a leak. They awoke to a sagging living room ceiling and almost as much damage. Just be aware that Murphy can visit your cache no matter where it's hidden.

Hidden Rooms

One of my editors purchased a home some years ago, surviving the gauntlet of inspections, mortgage paperwork, and the severe beating suffered by his bank account.

Weeks after moving in and unpacking, he discovered a heretofore unknown feature of the new abode.

Do you see anything unusual about this built-in shelving in the master closet?

Much to his surprise, it contained a hidden area large enough to store a significant amount of supplies, Christmas presents, or storage boxes.

"We moved in, unpacked, hung clothes in the closet and were in that area at least once a day. I never noticed it until I was installing some new hangers and spied a small gap between the door and the wall."

This example of a hidden room won't protect the contents from fire, a police dog, or even a methodical search. It most likely would foil all but the most observant thieves and looters and definitely keep your nosey neighbors and family members from spotting your prepper supplies.

As with most things associated with prepping, it could be enhanced at some expense. Fireproofing the interior would be one project, adding a hidden locking mechanism might be another.

I recently discovered a "secret room," in my own home, although I'm sure it was unintentional. More of a construction mistake, I'd say. After living in the same residence for over 15 years, I was in the far corner of the attic one day and noticed a two-foot wide section of missing insulation. When I crawled over to investigate, I was quite shocked to discover a canyon-like gap between a guest bathroom and an adjoining hall. This area was completely inaccessible from inside the home, and the space wasn't obvious at all. Yet, it was reasonably large, at 3-feet wide, 11-feet long, and 9-feet deep. I could put several years' worth of supplies in the space, and nothing short of demolition or a dog's nose would ever find it.

Like most "hidden rooms," the above two examples aren't going to fool a canine's snout or a determined search. They do, however, provide ease of access and a high level of security, at least while someone is home. If your dwelling isn't already equipped with a suitable space, constructing such a facility could be expensive.

Bunkers, root cellars, tornado shelters, and other subterranean, in-home options are also common in certain parts of the country. Some are even cleverly disguised and difficult to spot. These facilities generally fall into the category of a fallout, or bug-out location unto themselves, and will not be covered in this work.

ABOVE GROUND OPTIONS

Inside caves, caverns, and quarries. Deep caves make great placement for caches. Research the fragility of the structures, which could prevent future retrieval, as well as the animals and humidity within them that could damage the cache. If there's water, place the container as far away from it as possible.

People like to explore caves. If there is public access to the surrounding property, you might consider burying or covering the cache within the cave or cavern. If the walls have been spray-painted with graffiti, or there are piles of beer cans or used condoms inside, it might not be a good choice. If it looks like the site is seldom visited, a pile of heavy rocks might do the job of disguising your container.

Another option would be to find a natural indentation in the rock floor, insert your container, and then hard-pack matching dirt over the stash.

If the cave is small enough, disguise the opening, or even block it a large boulder. Consider using a winch, tractor, or truck to move the obstruction and block the entrance. Always keep in mind, you'll want to go back at some point.

Under Big Rocks. This is one of my favorite hiding spots in the desert around my western BOL. Since you don't want to crush your container or your skull, be extra careful using the following techniques.

A small, inexpensive hydropic tire jack for your car is an extremely powerful, compact tool for moving certain rocks. It's quiet and can be carried to the cache site without attracting attention. Throw in a couple of sections of 2x4 lumber for braces, and you'll be surprised at the size of rock that can be tilted or angled enough to dig out a hole for your cache. Again, extreme caution should be used to avoid injury.

I look for a flat, large "flagstone" type of formation, but the technique can be used for landscaping boulders, stone walkways, or any sort of heavy rock. Never stick anything but your shovel handle underneath a heavy, jacked item.

Once you scrape out enough soil to properly protect your container, lower its "headstone" back into place. You'll have an excellent cache.

Inside abandoned buildings. Observe the surroundings of the chosen building – if it's especially isolated, or near an area with low traffic, this might work. A building in a busy town or city may risk discovery. Some buildings may house criminal activity, surveillance, or visitors.

These sites are always tricky. If someone still owns the property or the authorities have seized ownership, entering the building may constitute the crime of breaking and entering. The structure could also be hazardous with obstacles such as unstable conditions, hidden asbestos, mold, fungi, and other substances, gang and criminal activity, dangerous animals, and more. Only consider this option if you know for sure that the building is unassociated. Consider personal protection, such as a weapon and hardhat, during placement, retrieval, and checkups.

Under or near abandoned railroad lines. The laws in your state may prevent trespassing for *all* lines, regardless of whether or not they're used. The cache could also be damaged from others trespassing or hiking along the abandoned tracks. Take precautions when considering this option, and find out more information about the railroad line you're interested in.

Your office building, factory, or place of employment. If you're very familiar and the right circumstances exist, this might be an excellent option for a small cache that doesn't contain controversial items such as weapons. A locking file cabinet, desk, locker, or other personal space might provide the urban prepper with peace of mind. Perhaps there's a well-hidden cubbyhole at the back of the warehouse, or maybe your boss is a prepper, too.

Any location that you visit regularly, and thus have good reason to be there, can be a potential for a cache site if you can avoid discovery by others. Of course, no one should risk a paycheck for a cache… that's just stupid.

SUBMERSION

Another method to consider is submersion, or storing the cache underwater. However, this requires as much thought and planning as burial – if not more. It also requires high quality and heavy-duty equipment for submersion, retrieval, protection, waterproofing, and resistance to high amounts of water pressure. With that said, it's an option to consider if none of the above options are possible or if the underwater locations you have in mind are better. Good underwater spots for caches are hard to find and can be even harder to relocate for retrieval and checkups.

Any underwater spot will require extensive study to determine the depth of water, pressure, and characteristics. Is it salty? Swampy? What are the surroundings, wildlife, weather patterns, and accessibility from the shore? Can you get there without crossing someone else's property? What is the type of bottom and how strong are any currents or tides? Is it fished regularly?

You will also want to be aware of possible nearby witnesses like wardens, fishermen, and campers along the shoreline. Sometimes this type of information can be difficult for civilians to obtain, especially if you're not a specialist with that kind of access. Obtaining it could even make you look suspicious.

Still, there are some excellent underwater cache locations.

For years, my family has enjoyed recreational boating. Our small cabin cruiser was a dedicated salt-water boat, complete with its own slip at a local marina. During that period of our lives, our mini-yacht was our bug out location for anything other than an approaching hurricane.

While the boat itself wasn't a prime candidate for a secret cache due to the prevalence of break-ins, the marina was. If you're familiar with such places, you know that the piers are cluttered with dock lines, ropes, submerged bait boxes, and other items. A sunken, waterproof container secured to the underside of the gangway would be very difficult to detect. Retrieval would have been as simple as pulling up the line after your dock mates were in their berths, or during weekdays when the place was typically abandoned.

There are, however, a unique set of risks involved with such a cache.

Occasionally, if a neighboring boat was experiencing some sort of hull or propeller issue, divers would be in the water. If the surrounding ocean/lake is clear, they might notice your line and container and become curious.

Another potential issue would be a hurricane or other significant storm damaging the pier.

It's not as easy to submerge something as you might think. Part of your container's space might be consumed with lead weights or other heavy ballast. One idea that comes to mind is the use of old, lead, plastic-covered barbell weights. They are weighty, compact, and very inexpensive.

Salt water is tough on equipment, so special attention must be given to the container materials, as well as the mooring lines. Personally, I wouldn't consider anything but a PVC vessel for a sub-sea hoard. Many boat slips have submerged plumbing lines for dockside water and electricity. Check the materials used for that specific environment and create your cache container out of similar stock.

Many marine supply stores offer specialized chain and rope designed to survive extended periods submerged. Galvanized anchor chain is available, as well as special dock lines that can withstand thousands of pounds of stress.

Our marina offered on-site, secured, storage lockers as well. These were normally filled with "boat junk," such as cleaning supplies, extra life jackets, and other discarded water toys. In our case, this would have been an excellent place to hide a cache.

Even if your nautical experience is limited to the occasional outing on a bass boat or canoe, you can still find excellent places to secure an underwater stash.

Small farm ponds or other manmade lakes can offer a variety of secure cache sites. The key is avoiding discovery by curious snorkelers, divers, or the occasional swimmer who jams his toe on your submerged container. Fishermen are famous for pulling up everything from dead bodies to old tires. You don't want them adding your cache to their catalog of lies and exaggerations.

I highly recommend avoiding any sort of moving water, including rivers, active tidal basins, or any body of water that experiences strong currents. Our marina was protected, and while a mild tide did occur, I wouldn't be concerned about having my AR and ammo pulled out to sea, even if the securing line did break. The tide just wasn't strong enough to move a weighted, sunken container. The bottom was mostly sand, so silting over short periods wasn't a worry.

Another factor to consider is freezing. If you live in a region where ponds and lakes typically freeze, you might want to go with another type of cache. You never know when you'll need those supplies, and chipping through a foot of ice doesn't sound like all that much fun.

Submersed Cache Success Story

A good tutorial for an underwater cache is found on *National Geographic*'s website, written by Survivor Jane and Rick Austin: It includes everything you need, from instructions and a step-by-step process to a list of equipment with prices and where to purchase. There is also a sample list of possible items to consider including in your cache. The article describes how to "decorate" a PVC pipe for easy submersion and retrieval.

Mooring

By far the easiest way to retrieve a sunken treasure is via a mooring line. You'll need at least one mooring line of sturdy material, maybe more, depending on the size and weight of your cache. Some common mooring lines include sisal fiber lines, nylon, hemp, polyethylene, and polypropylene. Fishing line of extreme breaking limits is an excellent choice. You can also use paracord, in fresh water.

You can either place heavy weights inside the container or attach the ballast on as an external anchor. If you don't want to lose that precious internal space, there are grapnel anchors that will be more than sufficient for your cache and are designed to be submerged for long periods. They're typically used for small boats, come in a variety of weights, and are inexpensive, depending on where you look. Check marine supply stores for lines and anchors or try eBay and online marine suppliers. Household scrap-iron or other heavy objects can rust quickly and allow your stash to float away or become visible on the surface.

Always keep in mind that you're going to have to retrieve that container at some point in the future, and it may have settled in bottom mud or have filled with water if the seal has failed. Both of these situations mean the weight of the cache has increased since you left it. Don't underestimate the capacity of your mooring line, or you might end up snorkeling or hiring a diver to retrieve your goodies.

Securing the mooring line would be the next consideration. You can tie your lines to a sturdy object, like a big tree, or a bridge support close to the submersion site. You can bury the line for concealment, attach to a pier, drain pipe, or other permanent structure. Be aware of curious people pulling in the line to see what's on the other end.

There is also buoy mooring. Here, the line is run from the container to a buoy or other floating marker. This will work if the submersion site is well isolated. I only recommend this on small, private ponds with no current or flow. When I was a kid, I used to walk the banks of local fishing holes, collecting discarded lures and bobbers. I would have found your cache.

Submersion Tips
- Your cache may be buoyant, even when heavy and filled to the brim. Make sure it's weighted sufficiently, and it stays in place. This may require some trial and error. Take note of the container's dimensions and its weight before and after placement of its planned contents. The depth at the submersion site will also impact the amount of ballast required.
- The greater the depth of the submersion site, the greater the amount of water pressure. Consider a container resistant to high amounts of pressure. Waterproofing also increases in difficulty. If you've ever been involved in the acquisition of a quality watch or have purchased optics, you'll see various water "resistance" standards listed in their features. "This watch

is water resistant to 30 meters for 60 minutes," or similar. There are military standards, ISO benchmarks, and an assortment of different measurements. Out of all this, the caching prepper needs to understand that water, under pressure, will penetrate minute gaps that ground water and moist soil cannot.

.

CHAPTER 13

DECEPTION, DECOYS, AND DISGUISE

We have touched on the idea of deception occasionally throughout this guide, and we will go deeper in this next chapter. I am dedicating an entire section to deception because it deals with more than digging the hole. Having deception in mind from the very beginning of your cache is a key to success. The worst-case situation is a thief can quickly become a predator if he or she uncovers your weapons and ammo; the best case is only a few cans of beans being stolen.

The concept can involve minor details and small acts on the part of the prepper. A minor example would be camouflaging your dig site. Too many acorns or piles of leaves will draw attention to the area. The same goes if your topsoil is dirt, and a large circle of clay is visible after you fill the hole.

They say the devil is in the details, and that logic applies with caches.

You always face the chance of losing a cache. A one hundred percent guarantee does not exist in this area of survival preparedness. We should always plan to anticipate the absolute worst possible scenario. So plan to lose a cache and know how to minimize the effects of the loss. This ties into deception in a few key ways, and that's why it's included in this section.

The first and most basic method to prepare to lose a cache is to create more than one stash, more than two, and probably more than three. Your cache should never be expansive. Never use a large cache to store tons of small items. This amplifies the risk of losing a large amount of investment and hard-earned cash.

If you can afford it and are willing, duplicate caches are an excellent way to hedge your bet. Food caches aren't an overly high expense in most cases, so why not have redundant supplies? Important survival gear, like prescription medications or antibiotics, should most definitely be replicated if at all possible. The "jack of all trades" hoard is one that contains a little bit of everything; these can easily be scattered here and there.

Duplicating any kind of firearm cache is going to be expensive, so that's why I recommend storing only one to two guns per cache. If you're only burying two weapons, split them into two caches.

Losing any property can be devastating, but it can and very well may happen. The wise prepper accepts this possibility up front and incorporates the risk into the plans, division of supplies, and alternatives.

Medical supplies, especially antibiotics, will save more lives than a gun will in a long-term SHTF situation. A thousand rounds of 5.56 can't fight off the common cold. The vast majority of medical supplies will have not a single trace of metal in them. So why store them with metal items and put them at risk of a metal detector?

Separating metal and non-metal containers will greatly improve the chances of your nonmetal items going undetected. Many times, we assign an overwhelming value on our metal items, especially firearms and tools. In a way, they are incredibly important, but they are not everything to survival. A length of parachute cord or fishing line could be more valuable than your AR 15 in the right situation. Everything is important. If it weren't, why bother caching it in the first place?

While the forward thinking prepper is always aware that the cache can be lost, that doesn't mean we get lethargic or simply throw our hands in the air.

There are steps we can take to reduce the risk of loss.

DECEPTION

A healthy dose of paranoia is well, healthy. Deception plays a key role in the overall effectiveness of a survival cache plan. Disasters and SHTF situations have the ability to bring out the best and the worst in people. You can see this with the yin and yang of volunteers helping, and the looters rampaging. This trait also manifests itself in the manner some stores gouge the prices of things like water while others simply give away emergency supplies during a crisis. People can be both wonderful and evil – why take the chance that your day will be ruined by the latter?

The idea that everyone who is knowledgeable about survival and prepping is a benevolent soul is a foolish notion. While my experience indicates that the vast majority are quality individuals; many of us are smart enough to be cunning as well.

Inevitably, some of humanity will become ruthless, another sect most likely to become desperate. These people read the same things you do; they prepare the same way. They will know about survival caches.

People you may consider friends or neighbors may be perfectly willing to rob you if they become desperate. These associates may know that you're a prepper. Right now, they may even consider you as the local weirdo. When the SHTF they may arrive on your doorstep with open arms and empty stomachs. The moral dilemma you face will be your own, and I cannot advise you on this. I can tell you once these people become desperate they may stop asking and start taking.

Operational security is a term the military uses quite frequently. OPSEC is a familiar acronym to anyone who has ever served. Essentially, it means never letting details escape about operations, regardless of how mundane they are. As an example, while one of the co-authors was in the Marine Corps, his wife attended a class emphasizing the importance of not revealing the slightest details of a deployment. The term loose lips sink ships is referring to OPSEC. Take this same idea with your cache. This is your first line deception - keeping your mouth shut.

I don't just mean keeping the cache's location a secret - that is obvious. I mean you should never even reveal your intent to

create one or even that you have the knowledge to execute such a thing. This is incredibly important as someone pointing a gun at you is going to ferret out your cache location if a criminal knows you have one. I advise not even telling your own family as the gun may be pointed at one of them.

The same logic applies to every step of the process. When burying, always have an excuse ready should your digging be discovered. One of my favorites: "My kid is doing a time capsule project for school." Don't lie to the cops, just take the fifth and keep your mouth shut.

"I'm doing repairs, installing a new drain..." These are all perfectly suitable answers to any unsuspecting passersby. You can even take your metal detector along and pretend you're digging something up. It's a great excuse for parading around the woods with a shovel and tarp.

The best OPSEC is not being seen at all. Digging in the middle of the night will look incredibly suspicious if your neighbor is out walking their dog and happens to spy your guilty looking, soiled body humping shovels of dirt at 3 am. I can almost guarantee a patrolling deputy will arrive and ask a few questions.

I suggest using an explainable time, such as sunrise on a weekday. Most people will be asleep, and for those awake it can be explained as simply yard work and beating the heat.

The next step is utilizing your location to aid in deception. We touched on this in the previous chapter, how site selection can be incredibly important. There are factors you can utilize to aid in the deception, and if possible, these should be tied into your location selection.

Little factors can make a big difference. Utilize a fence line when burying your cache. This aids in deception and makes it easy to remember where you buried your cache. The area a fence lies on is bound to be littered with small nails, staples, scraps of fence; things like this will make a metal detector go crazy. The presence of the fence, even above ground has the ability to give false positives to a metal detector.

The psychological aspect of the fence is another roadblock. A fence simply doesn't seem like an area to bury something. A fence is often perceived as a barrier, both mental and physical. That might just be enough to fool the narrow-minded thief.

Another potential advantage when it comes to property lines involves search warrants. These are typically restricted to your property - not your neighbors. This may make using a fence incredibly valuable in the face of overreaching authorities.

DECOYS

Decoys, oh decoys, the hassle they can create for the thief. A decoy is a passive way to confuse a foe, be they the authorities or a crook. It's all part of deception and protecting what's yours. Building and placing a decoy can give a thief a grin, but only a small one. The purpose of the decoy is to simply satisfy the criminal and send him on his way.

It's easy to picture the thief as a shady individual who is only out for himself and is most likely an evil presence. This will not always be true in a SHTF situation. More often, the 'thief' will be a desperate, hungry soul, who very well may be trying to provide for his family. I'm not trying to vindicate a criminal. I am trying to explain his or her motives. The contents of your decoy may save this struggling individual if it's found.

A decoy should contain nothing more than a few basic necessities. A couple of cans of beans or vegetables, maybe even a single MRE. Small items like Band-Aids, ace wrap, and Neosporin are inexpensive and can satisfy a desperate individual. The contents in a decoy should be realistic enough to satisfy a looter but inexpensive enough to be a viable feint. This fake-cache should also be available to supplement your supplies if it's never found.

The placement of a decoy is essential, akin to the lazy man's effort at hiding a cache. When thinking about a "head fake," take the advice throughout this book and forget about it. Bury it in an area that's noticeable, even leave a marking, nothing too obvious or it will seem like a decoy. An X carved into a tree is a good way to go. Like pirate lore of old, the X is the universal "Marks the spot signal," and is not a neon sign saying, "Dig here."

Having a decoy that is discovered and stolen can tell you a lot, much of which you might not have ever discovered without the deception. Finding your worthless cache has gone missing indicates folks may be onto you. They know you are a survivor and a prepper. You are also dealing with someone with enough education about survivalists to realize that people bury goods.

Now, you can recognize a potential hazard and adjust yourself to the situation. Now, you know you have a predator, and your security is going to have to improve.

ACTIVE DECEPTION

Active deception is where you are taking a stance in protecting your caches. This usually involves the placement of caches containing metallic items. Deceiving metal detectors, which are the bane of caches, is critical to your hoard's survival.

The art of active deception comes into play at every step of your planning. It ranges from identifying the threats to discouraging individuals from making off with your supplies.

A good place to start is to ask, "What are you hiding, and who are you hiding it from?" Food caches are always going to be at risk from individuals, but at no risk from tyrannical governments. Firearms, though, warrant the utmost scrutiny.

One simple example of active deception is to spread a layer of useless items above a deeper cache. These materials are basically anything that will aid in concealment or make digging up your cache difficult.

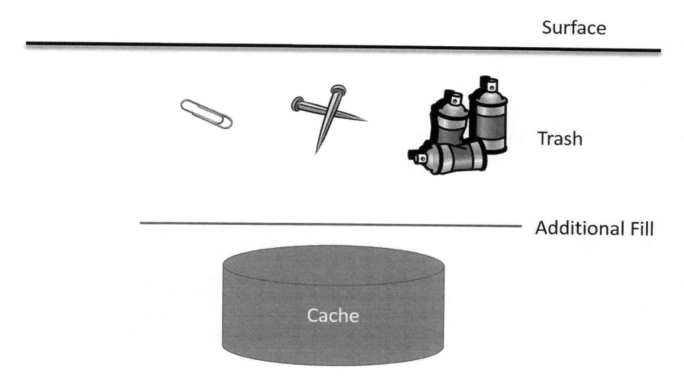

Surface

Trash

Additional Fill

Cache

The intent is to allow a scavenger or innocent treasure hunter to find the trash and stop digging.

Nonmetal caches do a lot of work for you; being immune to metal detectors is a major plus. One of the best things you can do for a pipe based, nonmetal cache is to make it look unappealing. Attaching extra PVC pipe to the ends of your cache can simply make it look like an abandoned pipe. Extra pipe means extra digging for you, but may be well worth it.

Essentially the middle pipe will be your waterproofed cache, with the end caps cemented down. The extra pipe will be added to the ends and lightly glued or cemented; it's important that you can still remove the extra pipe without too much effort. These hollowed ends will give it the appearance that it's simply an old pipe, or that it is still connected and running water. An extra, "Stay away from me," trick would be to write 'Septic' several times throughout the length of the pipe.

You could also bury a length of nasty-looking electrical cable a few inches above your cache. No one wants to fool with high voltage wires, and most likely would stop digging at that point. A fake gas line would surely invoke a similar response.

If you're in a remote area where it wouldn't make sense for pipe or cable to be in use, you'll need to disguise it as just abandoned trash. Making cuts in the extra pipe, or even breaking things like the ends off – anything extra you can do to simply make it appear as garbage. No treasure here; move along.

Another tip would be to add ferric chloride to the soil in the concealment site area. This can ward off metal detectors. It's used at Gettysburg battlefield to throw off potential treasure hunters.

Does your BOL have its own burial ground for processed animals? Is there a spot where the bones and other unused parts of deer, hog, or other game animal are buried or left to nature? Who wants to treasure hunt or scavenge there?

DISGUISE

Does your BOL have an outhouse? I bet most cache looters wouldn't want to go digging around under there. The same applies to my trash pit mentioned above.

What about a manure pile? Animal processing area? Hog pen?

Even desperate people have a sense of smell and some level of personal reserve. Hiding your goodies where potential crooks don't want to look or go can be effective if such options are available.

As mentioned above, high voltage electricity scares the hell out of most folks, myself included. If you're in an urban area, could you hide your cache in a fake utility box with those brazen yellow warning stickers all over the exterior? Who would look inside, other than a utility repairman? How often are they on your condo's roof?

Stickers, signs, and warning labels can be the sneaky prepper's friend. Gas lines, sewage pipes, toxic waste disposal… anything that would make a potential thief scowl and move on could be effective. Could you fill a fake pipe with supplies, label it "Chemical Waste Drainage," and hide it in the rubble of a collapsed building?

Prepper ingenuity and creativity never ceases to amaze me. Use those same creative brain cells when it comes to a cache, and you'll have a more secure future.

CHAPTER 14

FINDING YOUR CACHE

After you've gone to all the trouble scouting, waterproofing, digging, mooring, and camouflaging, now you need to ensure you can find that cache. If you have followed our advice and have multiple stashes, this may be more difficult than you think. If your cache is effectively camouflaged, the problem can be compounded. When an infantry unit is mapping a machine gun range card for a defensive position, we are taught never to use trees as targets because they always look the same. The same applies to 'remembering' the tree that marks your cache.

In some situations, using a tree can be an effective way to mark your cache if you're incredibly familiar with your area. This could work with a lone tree in a field or an oak tree in a forest of pines. There are always exceptions, but, in general, it is not good practice. Besides, trees can be cut, blown, and burned down.

The simplest way is to keep a handwritten note. These instructions shouldn't be too specific and should be kept close at hand. Being too specific could give too clear-cut directions to the wrong person if you misplace your note. An example would look something like this:

Start at A

Northwest corner

Count 10 from the corner.

Three paces further

Minus 2

Each line in this note is a distinct instruction. The first instruction is to stop at the A. The A could represent an intersection, two trees growing in a specific shape, or a sign with a dominant A in the lettering. This jump-off point needs to be something distinctive that catches your eye. The second instruction is easy; use points of direction instead of left and right to ensure that regardless of which way you're traveling the route it will be the same.

The third instruction is again coy, but easy to follow if you know the context. The cache is buried along a fence line, after the 10th post from the northwest corner. Now, three paces more, and that is where the treasure is buried.

Include odd phrases like, "From the promise, take six steps." What does that mean? This is where your distinct markings come into play. The promise is *John and Jayne Forever* carved into a tree. Utilizing a marking like these aids in the deception of both your note and lends a distinct marking. Minus two may seem confusing. Is it minus two from the six paces or minus two trees? Minus two refers to the depth of your hole.

"Minus 2" is two feet underground.

Your note doesn't have to look like mine at all. I wrote that as an example to give you an idea of what works.

An incredibly easy method to find your way to a remote landmark is via a GPS. I wore a Garmin wrist unit in Afghanistan for seven months and never had a problem with it. It has accompanied me to Romania, Africa, Spain, and the UAE. The downside to this is the battery; the Garmin product uses a rechargeable model. In a SHTF situation, this might be an issue. The Garmin is tough, waterproof, and is a great tool if you can keep it running.

GPS locations can vary up to several feet, so I don't recommend using it to pinpoint a hole. It can, however, be an extremely useful tool to verify you're looking at the correct radio tower, remote rock formation, or specific strand of trees used as a location marker or waypoint.

I also recommend having a backup method to find your way, such as a map. As much as I love the Garmin wrist GPS, I never put a 100 percent trust in any technology. Cell phones have similar capabilities, but if you're worried about governmental meddling, you won't take that smartphone along.

USING PLUMB LINES

One of my favorite ways to locate a buried cache is what I call plumb lines.

If there are two permanent features, such as the corner of the barn and the utility pole, stretch a length of paracord or fishing line between the two points and then measure footage or count paces. Make sure the anchors are likely to be around for years.

A similar approach is a virtual plumb line.

At one of my caches, there is a notch in a stone retaining wall. If I brace my favorite carbine in that gap and stand in a normal firing position, I'm looking at the cache in the cross hairs. If the weapon has an aiming laser, it illuminates the exact spot.

You could use nails on top of a fence post, a brace of wood at the corner of a building, or any other fixed pointing platform. A flashlight with a narrow beam could be used if you don't want to walk around with a weapon in hand.

Laser range finders are another excellent tool in helping pinpoint a hoard of goodies. Again, you're depending on technology, but it is extremely accurate and gives repeatable results. As an example, stand at a known, fixed position, such as a gate, tombstone, property marker, or utility pole. The graph below uses the corner of a barn.

With a second identifiable marker, such as the bridge, window, mountain, or radio tower as a directional pointer, focus the range finder until a set distance is displayed, such as 110 yards. This method only works if the line of sight is known, but it can be extremely quick and accurate to retrieve an otherwise non-descript cache.

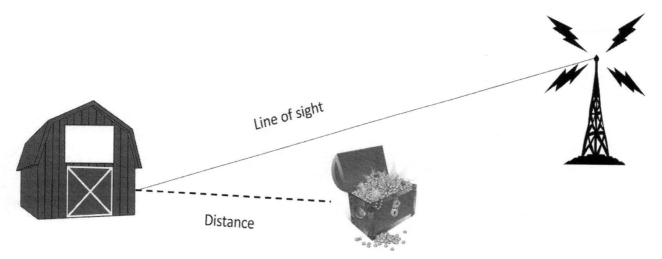

All of these techniques require detailed notes be taken at the time when you're hiding the cache.

As with all things committed to pen and paper, such evidence might come back and haunt you later. Such scribblings are poor OPSEC.

I suggest hiding your retrieval instructions in plain sight, such as embedded in a spreadsheet, inside your cell phone's contact lists, or another place where someone could be looking right at them and not realizing what they were seeing. Under no circumstances should you label such things, "Cache One, North Ranch," or similar.

Having a map covered with bright red "Xs" would be just as bad.

GOING HIGH TECH

At first, it may seem a bit odd to discuss high tech devices when addressing such a primitive concept as a cache. Yet, as in so many aspects of modern life, having technology at your disposal may improve the effectiveness of your hoard.

In fact, once we began researching for little electronic helpers, the number of options and their utility were quite impressive. Practically every aspect of a cache, from humidity monitoring to location can be enhanced with circuits and chips.

For example, the company EVA-DRY has a product (model ESS-E5550) that allows the remote sensing of humidity. Designed for safes, it allows you to place a sensor inside of a container and monitor the interior moisture levels up to nine feet away via a handheld unit. While we have not tested the device in a cache, the fact that it works through the steel walls of a safe gives us some confidence that it would function inside of a buried or hidden cache container. It costs about $20.00.

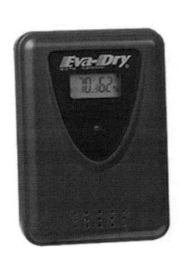

Such technology could save a lot of digging and the associated security risks involved in periodically checking your cache. With the EVA-DRY, or similar product, you would simple walk to within 9 feet of your stash and check the humidity level via the handheld remote. No shovel necessary.

There are some drawbacks, however. Both the sensor and display units require batteries. A call to the company's support line left us with the impression that the sensor (buried) should last 2-3 years with quality cells, depending on ambient temperature. We have not verified this claim.

Batteries aren't always a requirement. In fact, the variety of moisture detection meters, tools, materials, and sensors ranges from simple plastic strips that change color to sophisticated electronic meters that can run hundreds or thousands of dollars.

Many of the meters we investigated use various "probes" to measure moisture levels, which could be attached to the cache container's lid and avoid having to dig up the entire store and break a watertight seal.

If your stash is within range of a wireless hotspot, there are even more whizzbang gizmos that might enhance the security of your hoard.

Once such example is from Liberty, the gun safe manufacturer. They have a product designed to wirelessly monitor not only the interior humidity and temperature, but also alert you if someone moves your safe or opens the "door."

This black box works with smart phones and remote computers, allowing you to check the status "on demand." If someone opens your cache, it will even send you an alert.

Conceptually, it wouldn't be difficult to run a thin antenna wire from your container up a fence post, building wall, or tree to ensure good reception. If you're burying weapons and are concerned about someone discovering your goodies, this $200 option might be a worthy investment.

An economical option might be a simple humidity gauge, technically called a hygrometer. Millions of these inexpensive devices are used in households all across the planet, a standard part of any home weather station or outside thermostat. You've probably looked at one numerous times and never really paid that much attention.

Many of these units are available for less than $5.00 and are made of lightweight plastic.

With a PVC container equipped with a threaded cap, such an addition would be handy. Instead of excavating the entire cache for a maintenance check, you could uncover only as far as the lid and view the interior humidity without removing the entire casing. If your treasure is stored inside of a glass container, then just make sure to place the hygrometer near the top.

Gadgets such as these can also help with locating your cache or alert you if it's "on the move" due to discovery or theft.

Originally designed to track corporate shipments, a quick internet search of the term "GPS package tracking," will display dozens of companies that provide this very robust technology.

One example, from Trackinapack, claims 36 months of battery life on a single charge. You can view the unit's location from your home PC, which means checking that your cache is still where you left it no longer requires the expense and risk of visiting its location with a shovel in hand. Many of these gadgets are waterproof. They are also expensive, at $200-$300 each as of this writing, but prices are in decline.

If your cache contains a $2,000 worth of weapon, optic, ammo, and other gear, this level of investment might provide a worthy piece of mind.

Then there's Bluetooth technology, which is much more affordable. One of my favorite products in this category is called the "SticknFind." This button-sized device can be attached to car keys, cell phones, briefcases, and even luggage. The battery lasts about a year, which may be problem for some caches. Using your smartphone and a downloadable app called the "Radar Screen," you can hone in on your cache's location. Less than $50.00.

Pebblebee is a similar button-shaped device that has a three-year battery and a range of up to 150 feet. It is advertised as being water resistant, and even has a temperature-monitoring sensor. $16-40 bucks.

Bluetooth tracking is a growing industry, with new product announcements occurring frequently. Some of these new offerings will not only help you locate your stash, but also alert you if it is moving. Again, this could be an important security feature or help you find your missing tube of ammo if water washes away your PVC vessel.

Another option that is growing in popularity with tracking/finding items is RFID, or Radio Frequency Identification.

RFID chips are now in passports, credit cards, corporate identification badges, and even our pets. The Food and Drug administration has approved them for insertion into humans as well. Shudder.

As of this writing, the smallest RFID chip in the world was about the size of a speck of dust.

The range of RFID is typically quite limited unless the buyer is willing to spend significant amounts of hard-earned cash. Readers and proximity detectors with any range usable for locating a cache are hundreds of dollars for portable units. Still, the price continues to drop on this evolving technology.

Practically any electronic device will see its performance degraded by going underground, being submerged, or subjected to the interference of walls/structure. I would keep my purchase receipts and test as much as possible.

If you're like me, one of the biggest concerns with a cache is theft or losing your supplies/equipment. After that comes worrying about moisture and damage. Making periodic trips to verify that your assets haven't been discovered increases the risk that you'll be observed, or that someone will see evidence of your retrieval. For a few dollars more, the technology mentioned above can eliminate some of that stress.

CHAPTER 15

POSSIBLE SOLUTIONS FOR URBAN DWELLERS

So you live in a multi-unit apartment building or condo. You're surrounded by the proverbial concrete jungle. Where do you stash for the crash?

I have a friend who keeps a small cache at his gym in his private locker. It's one of those 24-hour places, always open and just a few blocks from his home. He can always get inside, day or night, and he feels like the security at the facility is sufficient to keep a small handgun, roll of cash, and other minimal "just in case," items safe.

There are gold prospecting organizations that are inexpensive to join (less than $100 per year) that provide members with access to thousands of "claims," or dig sites throughout North America. I belong to one. Over the years, I've found most of the members are preppers as well as 49ers. I've even seen Joe Nobody books for sale at their chapter meetings and campsite markets, so they must be good people.

If you've never tried it, prospecting with such a group can be a wonderful family outing. It's like camping and treasure hunting all combined. Some members don't even bother to pan for precious metals; they simply like towing in their campers and spending time with like-minded people.

If you were to join such an organization, you might find one of these isolated locales a workable option for your cache site. Members receive written permission to prospect on these claims, which means digging, camping, and more digging. You wouldn't look out of place driving up with shovels, supplies, and other tools required for burying a container.

Most of the claims I've visited are remote, with the primary activity being panning in a river or stream. Modern day prospectors use sophisticated metal detectors where they think gold may rest, so you should be extra careful to select an out-of-the-way spot to dig. Cover your tracks well.

The vast majority of members are weekend prospectors, so the various properties available are typically unoccupied on weekdays. As long as you maintain your membership, you should have legal access to the claim. Given the remote nature of these sites, I think this sort of arrangement is worthy of investigation if your other options are limited. You might even find some gold!

Long-term hunting leases are another possibility for those who don't own suitable real estate. These are essentially rental arrangements that allow you limited access to another's land while limiting the owner's liability. If you're unfamiliar with these legal agreements, there are all sorts of different options available, depending on what part of the country you reside. These can range from extremely costly "furnished hunts," to simpler, less expensive arrangements that allow primitive access to land for the purpose of taking game. At the high end, a lease can include guides, lodging, meals, and even ATV vehicles to reach the primary hunting areas. I don't recommend this sort of option for our purposes, and the cost is significant. Other options can be quite affordable.

While this suggestion contradicts our advice never to use land that doesn't belong to you, a multi-year lease can provide an additional level of "rights" to the property. Not the same as ownership to be certain, but far more than a common trespasser.

Some urban or suburban readers won't find any of the above options workable, either due to financial constraints, or geographical distances.

If you absolutely must hide your cache in a high-density population area, there still may be some workable options.

First, don't limit your thoughts to burial. Is there an area of the waterfront where you can submerge your cache and still retrieve it safely? How about rooftop access to your apartment building? Are there other rental options, such as storage facilities that you can access without having to produce identification? Lockers at a local community college may be for rent.

The rules for hiding a stash in a city are much the same as rural areas, low traffic, visibility, security against accidental discovery, and accessibility. As mentioned before, your mind is always the best prepper tool of all.

EMERGENCY CACHES

Some years ago, I was driving late at night, swerved to avoid a deer, and ran my pickup into a snow bank. It was stuck.

The forecast was calling for additional accumulation. The only civilization for miles was a small village that didn't even have a gas station, let alone a tow truck. There was no cell phone service.

The truck was safely off the road but going nowhere until I could find someone with a tractor or 4x4. That wasn't going to happen until at least daybreak.

Worse yet, I had two rifles in the bed of a 2-door pickup. There was no place in the truck to hide them, and I didn't think a stranger, walking through town carrying two weapons late at night, would elicit hospitable responses from the local population. Besides, I had a goodly amount of stuff in the cab that I didn't want to leave overnight or longer – depending on how bad the weather turned.

I thought about leaving my weapons on the floorboard given it was a low-crime, very rural area. That option, however, was soon dismissed, as it was just too tempting for anyone who might just happen upon it. Obviously, luck just wasn't with me that night.

Both blasters were in their original plastic cases, the cheap black ones that a lot of manufacturers ship with their product. I had a roll of duct tape in the cab. Lucky me… what rambling old pickup would ever be complete without a roll of duct tape?

Exhausted, pissed, and wanting nothing more than to get back to my friend's warm house, I decided on an emergency cache of sorts.

There wasn't much creative genius involved. I did my best to seal the non-waterproof plastic cases with the tape and then hide them under a bushy pine tree some distance off the road. I covered my snow-tracks as best as possible, loaded up my belongings from the cab, and began walking.

When I returned the following afternoon, courtesy of a nice local farmer and his Allis Chalmers tractor, I found my rifles right where I'd left them. The weather had turned warmer, some of the snow beginning to melt. While far from waterproof, my emergency cache had done its job well. Everything inside was nice and dry.

In a pinch, for short durations, several common items can be used to ensure temporary safekeeping of important kit. I could have used plastic trash bags (always in my bug out bag), or wrapped my rifles in a parka and taped the loose ends.

Like my little episode, there may be times where traveling with firearms, a big pack, or other man-portable survival gear isn't wise. You may not want to attract attention to yourself, or give any indication that you're a nomad of sorts. Local law enforcement can look upon armed vagabonds with a wary eye.

I've also experienced the need for a short-term cache while camping and rock climbing. I can't count the number of times I've felt insecure about leaving valuable supplies back at the campsite while we wandered into the rocks or mountains for a day of climbing. Yet, repacking everything and taking it with us on the trail cannot only be exhausting, but it also gets old.

Even if theft isn't a concern, bears, raccoons, and cats can be. The old trick of storing your food suspended from a tree really works – if there are any trees. I've gathered camp supplies into a parka and hid them in a tree or under a rock on several occasions.

CONCLUSION

Caching is a tried and true method of hiding critical items during difficult times. With clear thinking, a little common sense, and the instructions contained in this book, practically any prepper can increase security and peace of mind by creating one or more secret stores.

As with so many preps, I hope we never have to use our stashes. It would be just fine with me if at some point in the future, my grandchildren and I made a weekend out of digging them all up and having a good laugh at grandpa's paranoia.

Until then, I'm glad they're in place, secure, and available should the need arise. In a way, my hoards remind me of the smoke detectors in my home. Yeah, they cost a little bit. Changing the batteries is a pain, especially since I know that a very small percentage of homes actually catch on fire.

Still, I'm glad they're there.

See Joe Nobody's other books by visiting PrepperPress.com.

Made in the USA
San Bernardino, CA
25 August 2016